Teresa Hiers

Lady in Waiting

FOR THE PROMISES
OF GOD

TATE PUBLISHING
AND ENTERPRISES, LLC

Published by Tate Publishing & Enterprises, LLC
127 E. Trade Center Terrace | Mustang, Oklahoma 73064 USA
1.888.361.9473 | www.tatepublishing.com

Tate Publishing is committed to excellence in the publishing industry. The company reflects the philosophy established by the founders, based on Psalm 68:11,
"The Lord gave the word and great was the company of those who published it."

Book design copyright © 2011 by Tate Publishing, LLC. All rights reserved.
Cover design by Kenna Davis
Interior design by Lindsay B. Behrens

Published in the United States of America
ISBN: 978-1-61346-912-5
1. Religion / Christian Life / Women's Issues
2. Religion / Christian Life / Personal Growth
11.11.03

Dedication

$\mathcal{F}$irst and foremost, I give praise, honor, and glory to my God, my Lord and Savior, Jesus Christ, and to my Comforter, the Holy Spirit. Without the Trinity, I would be drifting through life aimlessly and without purpose.

Secondly, I want to thank by husband, Tom, who believed in me, and the purpose I was endeavoring to accomplish. His relentless support overwhelms my spirit. The encouragement he gave during times of sickness and the writing of this book was astounding.

Thanks be, unto God, for the mother and daddy, He entrusted to nurture and teach me the difference between right and wrong.

I also want to thank our families and friends, including our church family, for the labor of love and support through encouragement, and the prayer of intercession on our behalf.

Special thanks to Sharon Treadaway, who believed in me when I did not believe in myself. She is a mighty woman of God, and a powerful "prayer warrior"!

I would like to thank Cathy Williams, who was there for me, who helped me get back to life, after the death of my husband. Her love and compassion was instrumental in my healing process. She is a true friend indeed!

In addition, Benjamin Hall's expertise in acquiring the information in order to publish this book is very much appreciated.

Table of Contents

Foreword

Of course, God birthed this writing through prayer. Everything worthwhile is birthed through intimate relationship with Jesus Christ.

Several years ago, I felt in my spirit that, one day, I would like to write a book. It actually leaped out of my spirit during a work seminar, when I was asked to name a future goal for my life. I blurted out, "I want to write a book!" Well, as soon as I said it, I thought, "*Where on earth did that come from?*"

I now feel it was not from earth, but from heaven! Thinking back, it seemed as if the Holy Spirit leaped within me. I relate it to the time in the Bible when John the Baptist leaped in the womb of Elizabeth, when she saw Mary carrying our Lord and Savior, Jesus Christ.

Due to sickness of over six years, I had to quit my job. Please understand, God did not cause this infirmity to come upon me; but I do believe He allowed it for such a time as this.

My husband made the statement that maybe my purpose for being home was to prepare me for my destiny. One thing was sure, I now had the time for whatever the Lord purposed in His heart for me to accomplish. My belief is God took the plans of the enemy and turned them for good for His glory!

I completely forgot about writing a book until one day, during my prayer time, God reminded me of the desire to write. He laid it upon my heart, "Now is the time!" At this point, I did not have a clue as to what the topic would be.

Six days later, during prayer, God impressed upon me to write the vision and make it plain, as in Habakkuk 2:2-3. I obeyed, and then asked, "Father, what do you say about it?" Immediately, the words came to me, "lady in waiting." Whether it is the spouse God has chosen or His call on our lives, we are constantly in a state of waiting for something or someone. I knew, at that moment, God had given me part of the title of the book. You see, that is God's way; He only reveals a portion at a time. He wants to see, what you will do with the thing; He gave you! As you walk, He will reveal more and more.

Scripture began to flood my spirit like never before! The Holy Spirit amazed me with all He was bringing to my remembrance. Therefore, *Lady in Waiting: For the Promises of God* was birthed into existence.

We pray this book touches your life, so that it causes your life and the lives of your loved ones to be miraculously changed by the Spirit of God.

We would like to hear from you, whether it is through your testimony or your prayer requests. It would be our honor to pray earnestly for you. May God richly bless your life!

> Unto Him Who is able to do exceedingly, abundantly above all you could ask or think, according to the power; that worketh in you by Christ Jesus.
>
> Ephesians 3:20 (KJV)

> "For I know the plans I have for you," says the Lord. "They are plans for good and not evil, to give you a future and a hope, says the Lord."
>
> Jeremiah 29:11 (NKJV)

Introduction

Sharon Treadaway inspired the cover of this book through a vision she had, concerning me during a very difficult time in my life. She saw me laughing and dancing in a field of yellow flowers, with the wind blowing through my hair. I was adorned in a long, white dress. In the vision, there was a sense of me telling Satan, "Look at me now!" All the while, I was laughing and dancing, with hands raised, giving praise to God.

Sharon believes the Holy Spirit gave her the interpretation of the vision. What Satan meant for evil, God meant for good! The field is symbolic of the world, of God's work, and a harvest of a mixed multitude. The color, yellow, symbolizes gifts of feeling; gifts from or of, God, such as marriage, family, honor, and it, also means welcome home. Flowers mean glory, gifts, romance, and things, which are temporary in life. I was wearing a long, white dress, which meant a covering of anointing, protection, and authority. White is a symbol of purity: spotless, unblemished, blameless, righteousness, truth, innocence, and the bride of Christ; which is only possible through the blood of Jesus Christ. The hills or mountains mean a high place. The wind is a representation of the Holy Spirit gently, breathing over my life and guiding my footsteps. In the vision, it was, as if, I was being bathed in sunlight. The sun is a representation of the light, of Jesus Christ, the Son of God!

You will find throughout this book my thoughts and feelings about the rainbow. The rainbow is a very precious gift and has great meaning for me. It was created by God, as a sign to us, that He keeps His promises. Even the meaning of the rainbow is distorted in the world today. The rainbow was a necessary addition to the book, due to the fact; the rainbow is the reminder of the promises of God!

There are times, in all of our lives, when we do not see the presence of God flowing in our circumstances. He is like the wind; though you cannot see it, you can see the effects of it!

My hope for you is that the Spirit of God will flow through your life. Allow Him to take what Satan meant for evil, and turn it into good in your life as well!

Change of Heart

𝓜any of you are just starting out in life; but for many others, you are starting again. Then there are some who have started over, repeatedly. If you are just beginning or beginning again, God has a word for you.

> Trust in the Lord with all your heart; and lean not on your own understanding. In all your ways acknowledge Him and He shall direct your paths.
>
> Proverbs 3:5 (NKJV)

As my pastor says, all of our problems extend from sin. It does not matter what it is; it comes from sin. Whether it is sin of omission or sin of commission, it is still sin. Omission means it is from something we did not do that we should have done; commission means we did something that we should not have done. Your problems may not be caused by your sin, but by the sin of another. Unfortunately, the innocent suffer along with the guilty.

Usually, we enter into sin because we want to have it our way, like the old song Frank Sinatra sang, "I Did It My Way." Some of you may only remember the version of the same song by Elvis Presley. I am blessed to have lived long enough to remember both versions. The whole point being that is why we get into our sinful nature. This is where all our problems manifest.

You ask yourself, *Can I begin again in the right direction, with the right spirit? Is it possible to have a clean slate, a fresh new start?* The answer is, most definitely, yes! The Word says in Ezekiel:

> I will give you a new heart and put a new Spirit within you; I will take the heart of stone out of your flesh and give you a heart of flesh. I will put My Spirit within you and cause you to walk in My statutes, and you will keep My judgments and do them.
>
> Ezekiel 36:26-27 (NKJV)

By the way, this passage of scripture is very dear to my heart. I will explain this in more detail in another chapter.

Turn from the direction self is taking you. Turn back to your first love, if you have known the ways of the Lord. If you have not known Him, let this be an encouragement for you to turn to Him now. He has been there the whole time, lovingly, waiting patiently for you.

If you are, in fact, tired and disgusted with the way your life has been so far, it is time to make a change of heart. On the other hand, everything may seem like it is going well in your life, but there just seems to be something missing, a void in your life; then it is also time to make a change of heart. Notice I said make a change, because that is exactly what has to be done. You have to make it happen with God's help, of course. It is time to choose life and not death. Jesus Christ came that we might have life, and have life more abundant. He would not have us lacking in any good thing, because all good things come from the kingdom of God. Remember the model prayer Jesus gave us, "Our Father Who art in heaven, hallowed be Thy name. Thy kingdom come, Thy will be done on earth as it is in heaven." Therefore, we have the power and authority to loose whatever is in Heaven and bind up the things, which are not. You can find this in Matthew 18:18-19, read it for yourself. In addition, in Ephesians, it tells us the kind of life we can have if we are children of God.

> Now unto Him Who is able to do exceedingly abundantly above all that we ask or think, according to the power that works in us.
>
> Ephesians 3:20 (NKJV)

In return, for this abundant life, what does God require of you?

> He requires you to fear Him (reverent fear), to live according to His will, to love and worship Him with all your heart and soul, and obey the Lord's commands and laws that I am giving you today for your own good.
>
> Deuteronomy 10:12-13 (NKJV)

Did you get that last part? He says it is for your own good! It is not for the good of the Father, but it is to bring goodness into your life. God has already chosen you according to His Word in Deuteronomy, where He says:

> Yet, the Lord chose your ancestors as the objects of His love. And He chose you, their descendants, above every other nation, as is evident today. He tells us to cleanse our hearts and stop being stubborn.
>
> Deuteronomy 10:15-16 (NKJV)

In other words, now choose Him!
We also read in Psalm 51:

> Create in me a clean heart, O God. Renew a right Spirit within me. Do not banish me from Your Presence, and don't take Your Holy Spirit from me. Restore to me again the joy of Your salvation, and make me willing to obey You. Then I will teach Your ways to sinners, and they will return to You.
>
> Psalm 51:10-13 (NKJV)

We are born into sin; therefore, our nature is to please ourselves, rather than pleasing God. Through this passage of scripture, it shows us that David had a repentant heart. He asked for forgiveness for committing adultery and murder. God said David was a man after His own heart, because David was quick to repent.

> And when He had removed him (Saul), He raised up unto them David to be their king, to whom also He gave testimony and said, "I have found David, the son of Jesse, a man after Mine Own heart, who shall fulfill My will."
>
> Acts 13:22 (NKJV)

We must ask God to cleanse our hearts, just as David did.

Right actions and reactions can only come from a broken spirit and a repentant heart. "The sacrifices of God are a broken spirit, a broken and a contrite heart—These, oh God, You will not despise" (Psalm 51:17, NKJV). Only God can create a right or pure heart and spirit within you!

Do you feel broken? Are you brokenhearted? Sometimes, God allows our hearts to become broken in order to bring us to true repentance and to bring us back to Him. "He heals the brokenhearted, and binds up their wounds" (Psalm 147:3, NKJV). After all, we belonged to Him before we were ever born. He is our Creator.

> I knew you before I formed you in your mother's womb. Before you were born, I set you apart and appointed you as My spokesman to the world.
>
> Jeremiah 1:5 (NKJV)

You are probably saying to yourself right now, "*Yeah, well, He was talking to Jeremiah, not to me.*" That is where you are wrong. God is speaking to all of us. We are all His mouthpieces. We are to declare the works of the Lord, to proclaim the name of Jesus Christ. Our commission on this earth is stated in the book of Isaiah.

The Spirit of the Lord God is upon me, because He has anointed me to preach the good tidings to the poor; He has sent me to heal the brokenhearted, to proclaim liberty to the captives, and the opening of the prison to those who are bound; the acceptable year of the Lord, and the day of vengeance of our God; to comfort all who mourn in Zion, to give them beauty for ashes, the oil of joy for mourning, the garment of praise for the spirit of heaviness; that they may be called trees of righteousness, the planting of the Lord, that He may be glorified.

Isaiah 61:1-3 (NKJV)

Many times in the Word of God, it shows us examples of people who needed a change of attitude or mindset. It was not until God allowed their hearts to be broken through pain, suffering, and loss or defeat that their hearts turned back to God.

Take it from someone who knows, it is much easier to humble yourself before the Lord than to be humbled by Him.

God resists the proud; but gives grace to the humble. Therefore humble yourselves under the mighty hand of God, that He may exalt you in due time, casting all your care upon Him, for He cares for you.

1 Peter 5:5-6 (NKJV)

It is better to fall on the Rock (Jesus Christ) and be broken than the Rock fall and crush you.

Which do you choose: destruction or repentance? At times, unknowingly, I chose destruction because I was not in tune with the voice of God, or I was being rebellious and ignoring His voice. That is when you say, "God, I hear what You are saying; it sounds like a good plan, but I like my way better. I think it will work better this way. I will try it my way for a while; then if my plan does not work, I will try it Your way." At that very moment, you fall into a pit, not when the disaster hits. Trust me; it will blow up in your face eventually. You just set your path for destruction on the highway to hell!

Have you ever said, "It is my life; I will do what I want to do?" You might think it is your life and you are not hurting anyone else, but that is just simply not true. The real fact of the matter is you are hurting yourself, your future relationships, and everyone you care about or cares about you. Everything you do has an effect on those around you.

We only know what we see today, the circumstances or situations that affect us. We only see in part, and we do not see clearly.

> For now, we see in a mirror, dimly, but then face-to-face. Now I know in part; but then I shall know just as I also am known.
> 1 Corinthians 13:12 (NKJV)

Rest assured; God knows your life from beginning to end. After all, He is the Beginning and the End, the Alpha and the Omega!

> I am the Alpha and the Omega, the Beginning and the End," says the Lord, "Who is and Who was and Who is to come, the Almighty.
> Revelations 1:8 (NKJV)

Then, why do we not resign ourselves to the fact that only He knows what is best for us?

> Or what man is there among you who, if his son (or daughter) asks for bread, will give him a stone? Or if he asks for a fish, will give him a serpent? If you then, being evil, know how to give good gifts to your children, how much more will your Father Who is in Heaven give good things to those who ask Him!
> Matthew 7:10 (NKJV)

Trust in Him, surrender all to Him, and watch God miraculously transform your mourning into joy.

> For His anger is but for a moment, His favor is for life; Weeping may endure for a night, But joy comes in the morning.
>
> Psalm 30:5 (NKJV)

God has a divine plan designed especially for you. You are unique in every way; therefore, so is the plan He has for your life. I love the passage in Jeremiah where it says:

> For I know the plans I have for you," says the Lord. "They are plans for good and not for disaster (evil); to give you a future and a hope." "In those days when you pray, I will listen. If you look for Me in earnest, you will find Me, when you seek Me I will be found by you." says the Lord. "I will end your captivity and restore your fortunes. I will gather you out of the nations where I sent you and bring home again to your own land.
>
> Jeremiah 29:11-14 (NKJV)

Yes, God knows your future, and He holds it in His hands. His plans are for good and not evil, and they are full of hope, instead of hopelessness. He will gather us from our pits, bondages, strongholds, and from worldliness. Then, He can bring us into our promised land. Remember, it is Yahweh (meaning God's way), not your way!

Now, do you want God's plan for your life? Do you want a right heart and right spirit within you? If the answer is "Yes," then you are truly a "lady in waiting," ready to receive everything God has planned for you from the beginning of time. All you have to do is come before Him as a little child, asking the Father for a change of heart.

QUESTIONS FOR REFLECTION

Are you brokenhearted, if so, God can heal and restore you?

Can you honestly and without reservation say that Jesus Christ is your Lord and Savior? If He is not Lord and Savior of your life, are you willing to accept Him now?

Is the life you live pleasing to God?

What things can you do to make a change for the better in your life?

Do you sincerely want God's plan?

Are you ready and willing to do things God's way instead of your way?

Are you aware of God's purpose, calling and destiny for you?

Have you been obedient in walking out His plans?

PRAYER

Father,
I ask Your forgiveness from all my sin. As I humble myself before You, I ask that you cleanse me from all unrighteousness. Create a clean heart within me. Help me to love and worship You with my whole heart. I surrender my mind, will, body, emotions, relationships, and my finances to You, Lord. I accept You, Jesus, as my Lord and Savior. Reveal the destiny, calling and purpose You have for me. Thank you for strength and courage to trust the plans You have for my life, and to walk in them. By the blood of the Lord Jesus Christ, so be it unto me according to Your Word in Jesus Name. Amen.

I Will Arise

ℬeing curious, I looked up the words or phrase "I will" on Bible. com. The highest amount of scriptures it would pull up, for any phrase, was five hundred phrases. On this particular phrase, it recorded five hundred; but this only recorded scriptures from Genesis to Psalm 18:2. That is only about half of Bible scripture.

Among those were: "I will trust," "I will behold," "I will bless," "I will sing," "I will rejoice," "I will praise," "I will be glad," "I will come," "I will declare," "I will not be afraid," and "I will lay down in peace." All these are just the ones in Psalm chapter two through Psalm chapter eighteen.

Three scriptures actually say, "I will arise." Two of the scriptures, 2 Samuel 3:21 and Luke 15:18 were arising for good. The scripture in 2 Samuel 17:1 was for evil. The definition for "will" states it is a part of the mind that makes decisions with which somebody consciously decides things: the power to decide; to make decisions; a process of decision-making; a determination to do something; a desire or inclination to do something or to cause something to happen through attitudes, thoughts, or actions. The definition for "arise" means to occur; to happen; to come into existence because of something; to become active, vocal, or rebellious; to go up to a higher place or level, to sit up or stand up.

I will arise to repentance, to surrender, to acceptance of the Lord Jesus Christ. He is my Lord and Savior. I pray He is yours, too. I will arise to do the will of the Father. I will arise to what God called me to be. I will arise to the purpose and the destiny of my life. I will arise to trust, to love, to bless, to sing, to praise, to worship, to forgive, to be joyful, and thankful. I will arise to obtain all that God, the Father, has for me. I will arise to obtain all that Jesus, the Son, died for on the cross. I will arise for the anointing, authority, and the power of God, the Holy Spirit.

I Will Arise for Repentance

Repentance is for the remission of sins. When you read in Mark 1:4 and Luke 3:3, you will see the message of repentance. The message of repentance was a call to forsake your sins and to return to faithfulness in worship toward God. Repentance affects and effects the whole man. To affect means to influence, move emotionally, to infect or damage someone or something. Effect means a result; a change or changed state; the power to influence; bring in force, in operation, or the case, often from a particular point in time, impression, cause, or proclamation of an impression; a special sound or lighting. Affect is only a verb, whereas effect is both a noun and a verb. They both sound the same and have meanings that are closely related. It can be very confusing at times. If one thing affects another, it has an effect on it. You can affect (cause a change in) people or things; but you can only effect (bring about) things.

The actual meaning of repentance is to have a complete change of mind, a forsaking of one's past existence and an acceptance of a completely new approach to life. Therefore, repentance calls for an examination of oneself. The result is the recognition of your sins. Repentance also entails accepting Jesus Christ as your Lord and Savior. Then you will embrace a lifestyle that conforms to the likeness of Christ. "For Godly sorrow worketh repentance to salvation not to be repented of; but the sorrow of the world worketh as death" (2 Corinthians 7:10, KJV).

John the Baptist was talking about Jesus in the book of Matthew when he said:

> I indeed baptize you with water unto repentance; but He that cometh after me is mightier than I, whose shoes I am not worthy to bear. He shall baptize you with the Holy Ghost and with fire.
>
> Matthew 3:11 (KJV)

You may ask, "How do I repent?" This passage is from the heart of David:

> Have mercy upon me, O God, according to Thy loving kindness; according unto the multitude of Thy tender mercies, blot out my transgressions. Wash me thoroughly from mine iniquity and cleanse me from my sin. For I acknowledge my transgressions, and my sin is ever before me. Against Thee, Thee only, have I sinned and done this evil in Thy sight, that Thou highest be justified when Thou speakest, and be clear when Thou judgest. Behold, I was shaped in iniquity, and in sin did my mother conceive me. Behold, Thou desireth truth in my inward parts; in the hidden part Thou shalt make me to know wisdom. Purge me with hyssop, and I shall be clean; wash me, and I shall be whiter than snow.
>
> Psalm 51:1-7 (KJV)

Of course, you do not have to pray the exact way David prayed. You just have to pray from your heart of truth. Much joy resounds into heaven when one repents.

> I say unto you that likewise more joy shall be in heaven over one sinner that repenteth, than over ninety-and-nine just persons who need no repentance.
>
> Luke 15:7 (KJV)

I have sinned, you have sinned, and we have done things and will do things that will be in need of repentance and forgiveness. In fact, I have failed miserably at times. If not for God's love, grace, and mercy, where would we be? "For all have sinned and come short of the glory of God" (Romans 3:23, KJV).

I Will Arise for Forgiveness

The word "forgiveness" means the act of pardoning someone for a mistake or wrongdoing. It is the removal of sin (as far as the east is from the west), and restoration of the person or persons who are hurt by sin. In order to have true forgiveness, there has to be true repentance, which is a change of your mind, will, and emotions.

In a right relationship with God, there is also the need for repentance and forgiveness. Jesus taught us to be quick to forgive (before the sun goes down on your anger). He also taught us that our forgiveness should be without limit, which is the same way God forgives us. "Jesus saith unto him (Peter) I say not unto thee, until seven times: but, until seventy times seven" (Matthew 18:22, KJV). (Four hundred ninety times, and He was talking about for the same thing.) If we want or expect forgiveness from God for our sins, then we have to forgive others for their sins against someone we love or ourselves.

> For, if you forgive men their trespasses, your heavenly Father will also forgive you. But, if you forgive not men their trespasses, neither will your Father forgive your trespasses.
> Matthew 6:14 (KJV)

I have heard many people say, "Well, I may forgive them, but I will not forget it!" I have been guilty of that little speech, too. If that is your attitude, then you truly have not forgiven that person. When I am talking about forgetting, I am not saying you do not remember what happened. However, when you feel hatred, or anger rise up inside you, when you talk about the situation or about the person that hurt you, then you have not truly forgiven. In other words, you still criticize, condemn and hold a person or persons responsible for what they did to you or a loved one.

If you know of anyone you have not forgiven, including yourself, take this time to forgive. You may not feel anything change right now; but each time it rises up inside of you, ask God to help you forgive. After all, forgiveness is a decision you make, not a feeling. With Jesus, you are able to forgive. One day, you will notice the pain becoming less and less, until it is no longer there.

You may think, by not forgiving, you are hurting the person that hurt you. That is where you are wrong! The person you are hurting is yours truly. That is right, it hurts you! When you harbor these feelings in your heart, you are enabling the person who hurt you to have power over you. You only release that hold when you forgive. Not only do you give them power over you; but if you do not forgive, it can cause a root of bitterness. There is proof that bitterness can cause all kinds of diseases and sicknesses. Trust me; it is much easier to forgive than to go through life with bitterness. Remember, if you want healing from your past hurts, it starts with forgiveness. In fact, that is the only way it comes!

You see, when God forgives us, He says He remembers it no more. In other words, He does not hold that sin against you. Your slate or record is wiped clean; it is absolutely, spotless!

> I, even I, am He that blotted out thy transgressions for Mine Own sake, and will not remember thy sins.
> Isaiah 43:25 (KJV)

> As far as the east is from the west, so far hath He removed our transgressions from us.
> Psalm 103:12 (KJV)

It is forgotten! Remember, it was and is still commanded to for-give. This was not in an if-you-feel-like-it scenario! There are no exceptions to this rule.

> And be ye kind one to another, tender-hearted, forgiving one another, even as God for Christ's sake hath forgiven you.
>
> Ephesians 4:32 (KJV)

> Forebearing one another, and forgiving one another, if any man has a quarrel against any: even as Christ forgave you, so also do ye.
>
> Colossians 3:13 (KJV)

In addition, let us not forget the scripture about leaving your gift at the altar and seeking forgiveness, then giving the gift to God. We find this scripture in Matthew:

> Leave there your gift before the altar, and go your way; first be reconciled to your brother, and then come and offer your gift.
>
> Matthew 5:24 (KJV)

Do you see how important this is to God?

Moses prayed to God for forgiveness for others. He had so much compassion for God's people; he prayed that God would for-give them. It tells of this in Exodus:

> And Moses returned unto the Lord, and said, Oh, this people have sinned a great sin, and have made them gods of gold. Yet now, if Thou wilt forgive their sin: and if not, blot me, I pray thee, out of thy book, which Thou has written.
>
> Exodus 32:31-32 (KJV)

Do you have the compassion Moses had to pray for God's peo-ple today? Will you pray to our intercessor, Jesus Christ, to release

Him to pray for them? Do you have a compassion for the lost? On the other hand, do you only care about you and yours?

> Look upon mine affliction and my pain; and forgive all my sins.
>
> Psalm 25:18 (KJV)

> But there is forgiveness with Thee, that Thou mayest be feared.
>
> Psalm 130:4 (KJV)

> And forgive us our debts, as we forgive our debtors.
>
> Matthew 6:12 (NKJV)

All of the previous scriptures were about us asking God to forgive us and about us forgiving others. Many times, it is easy to ask for God's forgiveness and a little harder to ask for someone else to forgive you or you to forgive someone else, but it is a great deal harder to forgive ourselves. Sometimes, the hardest person to forgive is you! However, if God forgave you, what gives you the right not to forgive yourself?

If you do not forgive yourself, you cannot get pass the past: the past hurts, past pain, past suffering, and past failures. Stop living in the past; get on with the future. In Philippines, Paul writes:

> Brethren, I count not myself to have apprehended; but this one thing I do, forgetting those things, which are behind, and reaching forth unto those things, which are before. I press toward the mark for the prize of the high calling of God in Christ Jesus.
>
> Philippines 3:1-14 (KJV)

Emerge from the circumstances, situations, condemnation, sins and ungodly relationships that have held you captive. Instead, saturate yourself in God's love, grace, and mercy. Saturate your life with the Word of God, with godly relationships, with hopes, with God-given dreams, visions, and goals. God has greater things than you could ever imagine planned for you!

> Unto Him who is able to do exceedingly, abundantly above all that you could ask or think, according to the power that worketh in you.
>
> Ephesians 3:20 (KJV)

I am a witness, I can attest to the fact, this scripture is true in my life and the same can be true in your life as well. It is up to you whether or not you believe and receive it.

The promise of forgiveness is throughout the whole Bible. This particular passage is just one example:

> If my people, which are called by My name, shall humble themselves, and pray, and seek My face, and turn from their wicked ways: then will I hear from heaven, and will forgive their sin, and will heal their land.
>
> 2 Chronicles 7:14 (KJV)

There it is again, He does exceedingly, abundantly above all we could ask, think, or even imagine. He not only forgives us; but also look at all the fringed benefits that are available. God is awesome!

> If we confess our sins, He is faithful and just to forgive us our sins, and to cleanse us from all unrighteousness.
>
> 1 John 1:9 (KJV)

I cannot give you all the scripture on everything I am writing to you about; but it would be good for you to look up the scriptures for yourself. That way, it gets deep into your spirit.

I Will Arise for Salvation

What exactly is salvation? It is the protection, saving, or deliverance from harm, destruction, difficulty, failure, bondage, poverty, disease, distress, or sin. The type of salvation I am writing about can save you from an eternal hell of damnation. Salvation includes spirit, soul, and body. Salvation is the answer to all our problems, situations, and the answer to all our questions in life, now and for eternity.

We are in need of a savior! The only one qualified to be our Savior was and is, Jesus Christ. He made the supreme sacrifice. He laid down His life for us. It was not taken from Him; He gave His life freely. He died for your sins and mine. Through His death, He gives life, and life more abundant.

We are saved by grace, and not by our works, not by anything we could do in and of ourselves. Salvation is a precious gift for which Jesus Christ already paid the price. He paid the price by the sacrifice Jesus made on the cross over two thousand years ago. It is freely given to all who would ask and receive. "Being justified freely by His grace through the redemption that is in Christ Jesus" (Romans 3:24, KJV). Justified means just as if I had never sinned. That one statement right there should put joy and peace in your spirit.

> What a difference between our sin and God's generous gift of forgiveness. For this one man, Adam, brought death to many through his sin. However, this other man, Jesus Christ, brought forgiveness to many through God's bountiful gift. In addition, the result of God's gracious gift is very different from the result of that one man's sin. For Adam's sin led to condemnation; but we have the gift of acceptance by God, even though we are guilty of many sins. The sin of this one man, Adam, caused death to rule over us; but all who receive God's wonderful, gracious gift of righteousness will live in triumph over sin and death through this one man, Jesus Christ.
>
> Romans 5:15-17 (NLT)

But God is so rich in mercy, and He loved us so very much, that even while we were dead because of our sins, He gave us life when He raised Christ from the dead. (It is only by God's special favor that you are saved!) For He raised us from the dead along with Christ, and we are seated with Him in the heavenly realms—all because we are one with Christ Jesus. Therefore, God can always point to us as examples of the incredible wealth of His favor and kindness toward us, as shown in all He has done for us through Christ Jesus. God saved you by His special favor when you believed. Moreover, you cannot take credit for this; it is a gift from God. Salvation is not a reward for the good things we have done, so none of us can boast about it. For we are God's masterpiece, He has created us anew in Christ Jesus, so that we can do the good things He planned for us long ago.

Ephesians 2:4-10 (NLT)

He will hear you when you call. "Call unto Me and I will answer you and show you great and mighty things, which you know not" (Jeremiah 33:3, KJV). I have heard this scripture often referred to as God's telephone number. Some of you may remember the old song about Jesus on the main line, call Him up, and tell Him what you want. Well, now is your opportunity. What are you going to do with it? Just say, "I will arise for everything Jesus has for me, I will arise for everything Jesus died for on Calvary."

Remember, all we have to do is call on the name of the Lord Jesus Christ, repent for our sins, give, ask, receive forgiveness, and accept Jesus as our Lord and Savior. It is you who decides for what you will arise. You will become a new creature in Christ when you decide to do so.

I know that the majority of the women reading this book already have an intimate relationship with Jesus. For those of you who do not know Him as your personal Savior, or those who want to re-dedicate your life, now is an excellent time to turn everything you are and everything you ever want to become over to Him. Take some time to pause and reflect on the questions below. Then, will you humble your heart and pray the prayer provided or just talk to the Lord in your own way?

QUESTIONS FOR REFLECTION

What do you rise up for in the morning? Is it for good or evil?

Do you arise to do the will of the Father?

Are you pursuing all that God has for you?

Are you receiving everything Jesus died to give you, such as, salvation, healing, deliverance, protection and provision?

Do you have a heart; which is humble and repentant?

Have you forgiven all those who have hurt you or the ones you love?

Have you forgiven yourself for the mistakes and failures in the past?

Who or what has power over you; because you have not forgiven?

What can you do to make things right with God, with others and yourself?

PRAYER

Lord Jesus,
I repent of my sins, I ask for forgiveness and I receive that forgiveness. I make a commitment within myself, to enter into a covenant of forgiveness with those who have hurt me

or hurt the ones I love. I know, through forgiveness, You have my best interest at heart.

Jesus, I believe You were born of the Virgin Mary. I believe You died on the Cross for the remission of my sins, for my deliverance, for my provision, and I believe by Your stripes, I am healed in every area of my life. I relinquish all that I am and all I hope to be over to You. I believe You rose from the grave and You are sitting at the right hand of the Father making intercession for me. I thank You, Lord for all You have done, all You are doing, and all You are going to do, on my behalf. Amen.

For God so loved the world, that He gave His only begotten Son, that whosoever believeth in Him should not perish, but have everlasting life. For God sent not His Son into the world to condemn the world; but that the world through Him might be saved.

John 3:16-17 (KJV)

For the scripture saith, whosoever believeth on Him shall not be ashamed. For whosoever shall call upon the name of the Lord shall be saved.

Romans 10:11 (KJV)

Speaking From Experience

*T*hough you might be thinking I've had an easy run of things, rest assured I've faced some seemingly insurmountable struggles. I'm sure you have too. Let me just say, *if not for God*, I would be guilty, out of my mind, poverty stricken in every area of my life, disgusted, alone, lost in sin, dead, condemned, and on my way to hell.

Before I go any further into this chapter, please understand, I'm not writing this to get you to feel sorry for me in any way, form, or fashion. God brought me through numerous trials, as I am sure He will continue to do throughout my lifetime. He will do the same for you, also, because He is no respecter of persons. This is simply my testimony of His salvation, healing, deliverance, protection, and provision. This is my "Trophy Room." As you can clearly see, this is the longest chapter in the book. These testimonies are just a small portion of all the things in which God has sustained me. I hope that through the writing of this book, it will show you just how truly awesome God can be in your life as well. It does not matter what you have been through, what you are going through, or what you will go through in this lifetime; God is still God!

Guiltless

I thank my God my daddy never molested me. I thank God he was a very loving father to me. He made me feel like a little princess. Of course, I had the advantage of being the only girl among three younger brothers.

There were other people, that I should have been able to trust, but could not. Then there was also a total stranger. I remember an incident on one occasion, when I was probably twelve or thirteen years old. I was going to the neighborhood store, which was not out of the ordinary. We considered it safe back then, nothing compared to the way it is now. The store was about five blocks from our home, and this was a very heavily populated residential area.

My oldest brother was about ten, and the younger brother was approximately eight. I was pulling the youngest in a little red wagon when I noticed a van pulling off the side of the road. The man got out of his vehicle and went to the back of the van, where there were double doors. He proceeded to climb inside the doors. I really did not think anything about it until he started clearing his throat, continuously. I automatically turned my head toward him; as I did, I noticed he was standing inside the double doors. What I saw next totally shocked me. The man (if you can call him that) was exposing himself and making all sorts of vulgar gestures. At this point, I could get very descriptive about his actions; but I will spare you the details. The purpose in that particular statement is the fact that it is still vividly etched in my mind. From age twelve to age fifty-four, I still remember the fear that ignited within me.

After witnessing that vulgar display, all I can remember is that we were a block away from the grocery store. I took off running so fast and furiously; I almost threw my little brother out of the wagon. I was yelling at my other brother to run. He did not have a clue as to what was going on; but he came running after me. We made it to the store safely. I do not remember how long we stayed there, but when I was able to muster up the courage, we walked back home. I just remember being very terrified! More than likely, I prayed all the way home because, at the age of twelve, I accepted Jesus as my Lord and Savior, and I prayed frequently.

When we arrived home, I was very apprehensive about telling my mother. Finally, I scraped up enough courage to tell her what happened, begging her not to tell Daddy. She said she had to tell him. That frightened me even more. They both sat me down and talked with me, questioning me about the incident. I remember being very embarrassed talking about it.

Daddy asked me if I had done anything to provoke or encourage him to do this. This line of questioning caused hurt and rejection to set in me. The guilt and blame seemed to fall on me instead of this evil, perverted man. I am sure they had no comprehension of what just flooded my soul and spirit. My parents did not mean to harm me in any way. They were just trying to get to the bottom of this, so they would know how to handle it. At the time, I was still playing with dolls, for heaven's sake! What on earth could I have done to cause this? My answer to this question, and to those of you who have experienced this and far, far worse, is absolutely nothing! We did nothing wrong; it is not the fault of the child!

Daddy wanted me to describe the van and the man to him because he intended to conduct a search for him. Fear overwhelmed me; because if he did find him, I was afraid something would happen to my daddy. Then I would feel even more responsible.

Only recently, God brought the incident to my remembrance, and I came to the realization that I still harbored guilt and feelings of unworthiness inside my heart. Through the grace of God, I was even able to forgive the person that violated my innocence. I also forgave Daddy for the feelings of guilt, blame, and shame I felt, even though he had no knowledge of the hurt and he now is in heaven. You see, the forgiveness was not for his benefit and healing; it was for mine.

I thank God for His protection. This situation could have ended much worse than it did. I shudder to think of the possibilities that could have taken place, *if not for God.* Many times, situations like this have ended in horrific tragedy, leaving lives, utterly, destroyed.

Mothers, I implore you to listen attentively to your children. If they trust you enough to come to you, be attentive. At least pray about it, commune with the Holy Spirit. Then, if the Spirit confirms that something is not right, conduct your own investigation. You owe it to your children, and to others, to search out the truth and to stop the perpetrator.

QUESTIONS FOR REFLECTION

Have you ever been abused, molested, or raped?

Did you feel shame or guilt about a situation in which you had no control?

Are you still carrying the burden of shame, pain, and guilt due to the incident?

Have you forgiven all who were involved?

Have you confided in someone you can trust?

Have you asked God to cleanse your mind and emotions from the memory of those situations?

Writing is very helpful to me. It allows me to express my feelings by writing it down on a piece of paper. Writing releases all the negativity from your mind and emotions by transferring it to the paper, which is tangible. It is something you can actually see and touch. It helps you to express your feelings, vent your anger and hostility, rid yourself from all unhealthy emotions; which cleanses you spirit, soul and body, and then brings forth healing. Want you try this exercise for yourself? After you have done this, you need to pray over it and burn it if you like. I promise you will feel much lighter and refreshed.

PRAYER

Father,

I ask that You help me to find the strength and the courage to forgive those who have caused me so much pain and suffering. I pray that they will ask You for forgiveness for what they have done, and that they will never harm anyone else. I realize that by forgiving them, it does not condone or excuse their actions; but it releases me from their power and control. My forgiveness liberates me from all negative or evil works; which could cause sickness and disease. Deliver me from all shame, unworthiness and guilt. Renew my mind and my emotions in order to cleanse me from the memory of those situations. Help me to enter into Your peace and Your rest, to start each day fresh, leaving the things in the past far behind me. God, I ask that You take this attack against me and turn it for good so that it will bring glory to You. I am reminded of the scripture where it plainly states that if I do not forgive, I will not be forgiven. I do not want anything to come between Your forgiveness for me. All these things I ask in the name of Jesus. Amen.

You Shall Live and Not Die

At the age of eighteen, I nearly died. *If not for God,* I would have bled to death. I started my menstrual cycle and could not stop. I began to pass blood clots the size of oranges. I was afraid to tell my mother, because I was too modest and embarrassed to go to the doctor. To keep my mother from finding out, I would literally pack towels underneath me while I slept.

One day I became so weak, I could barely get out of bed. When I got up to go to the bathroom, I passed out. I found myself in the hospital for approximately a week. They had to give me three pints of blood. The doctor said I would have lain there and died in my sleep that very night. Thank God, I passed out when I did!

All because of fear, Satan nearly defeated me. God used my mother's prayers and the word of God as an instrument to protect and bring me to the fulfillment of God's plan for my life. She was able to lay fear aside and replace it with faith and God's Word. The scripture she stood upon is in Ezekiel: "And when I passed by you and saw you struggling in your own blood, I said to you in your blood, 'Live' (Ezekiel 16:6, NKJV). Because of fear, I could have lost my life; but because of faith, I received restoration and healing. I shall live and not die; I shall declare the works of the Lord!

You see, fear is one of the strongest tools Satan can use against you. If he can instill fear in any area of your life, if he can play with your mind and your emotions, then he can pretty much control your actions and your thoughts about any situation. Fear is a feeling of anxiety or apprehension, an unpleasant feeling or thought of distress, caused by the presence or anticipation of danger and worry. All of this is of the enemy. The Bible says, "For God has not given us a spirit of fear; but of power, and of love, and of a sound mind" (2 Timothy 1:7, NKJV).

The fear we are supposed to have is the fear of the Lord. This is to revere God, to show respect for or be in awe of God. In other words, we are to reverence God for His love, grace and His mercy.

Several scriptures talk about the fear of the Lord being wisdom. Here are three of them:

The fear of the Lord is the beginning of wisdom: a good understanding have all they that do His commandments: His praise endureth forever.

Psalm 111:10 (KJV)

The fear of the Lord is the beginning of knowledge: but fools despise wisdom and instruction.

Proverbs 1:7 (KJV)

The fear of the Lord is the beginning of wisdom, And the knowledge of the Holy One (Holy Spirit) is understanding.

Proverbs 9-10 (NKJV)

People are always searching for wisdom, knowledge, and understanding. They are usually looking in the wrong places. We are to look to God. After all, these attributes come from Him. These precious virtues do not come from fortune-tellers, soothsayers, Ouija boards, tarot cards, palm readers, séances, or false prophets. All of the above involve familiar spirits. Believe me; you do not want to have anything to do with familiar spirits. These spirits are not your loved ones that have died. They are demonic forces, plain and simple.

For the Lord giveth wisdom: out of His mouth cometh knowledge and understanding. He layeth up sound wisdom for the righteous: He is a buckler to them that walk uprightly.

Proverbs 2: 6-7 (KJV)

If any of you lack wisdom, let him ask of God, that giveth to all men liberally, and upbraided not; and it shall be given him.

James 1: 5 (KJV)

Remember how God blessed Solomon because he asked for wisdom to rule over his kingdom. Since he asked for wisdom, God added everything else to him, both great riches and honor. Solomon sought the kingdom: "But seek first the kingdom of God and His righteousness, and all these things shall be added to you" (Matthew 6:33, NKJV).

Miracle Birth

Due to all the female problems I had, the doctors said it would be next to impossible for me to get pregnant. Sometimes, I would only have one or two menstrual cycles a year. The doctors said I would have to take fertility drugs and have all sorts of tests in order to become pregnant.

If not for God, I would not have had the three precious children I have. You see, it was a miracle that I became pregnant in the first place. I had a daughter, and then eighteen months later, I had a son. It was not until almost eight years later, my youngest daughter was born. All of my children are very precious to me. All three of them, as all children are, were gifts from God.

If you have children, you will understand what I am about to say. If you have yet to become a mother, then here is some advice for you. I love them all the same, but differently. My attention seems to draw to the one who needs me the most at that particular time.

My oldest daughter, Mandi, was the first-born. She was born in December. What a wonderful Christmas we had that year, full of joy and happiness, with a ray of hope for the future.

When Mandi was about five weeks old, we almost lost her to double pneumonia. She was in the hospital for nine days. The first night, she almost died because the treatment they were using made it worse, instead of better. God intervened and totally restored her back to health.

When Mandi was five years old, Satan tried again to destroy her. I sent Mandi and her brother, Jesse, to ride their bicycles in the mobile home park where we lived, so that I could mow the grass. I thought I was protecting them. However, kids will be kids! As they were riding their bicycles, Mandi spotted a shiny quarter on the pavement. Of course, she stopped, picked it up, and tried to ride with the quarter in her hand. When this did not work very well, she decided to put the quarter in her mouth. On the way to the house, she hit a bump in the road, sending the quarter down her throat. She told me what had happened, and it was causing her throat to hurt. I called the hospital emergency room to find out what I needed to do in a situation like this. They were very calm about it and told me to see if she could eat or drink something. My mother-in-law told me to make her eat some bread and wash it down. My husband tried to make her throw it up. We tried everything and actually did think she had thrown up the quarter. I had a suspicion in my spirit that it was not over yet. That night she slept with us. I kept my hand on her chest all night long, making sure she was breathing properly. During the night, she started running a low-grade fever.

The next morning, I took her straight to the doctor's office. He even said, with all we did, she probably threw it up or she would pass it. I just was not at peace; therefore, I made the doctor do an X-ray on her throat. I wanted to know exactly where that quarter was, and I did not care if he had to x-ray her from head to toe!

The doctor ran back into the room and called the emergency room for them to set up the breathing equipment. He turned to me, telling me to get to the emergency room as fast as possible. Sure enough, he found the quarter through the X-ray. It was standing straight up and down in her windpipe. He explained that if she did not make it to the emergency room before the quarter falls, she might not make it at all, because the quarter would completely cover her windpipe.

They put her to sleep and removed the quarter surgically. The doctor said considering everything we did, it was a miracle the quarter did not fall, thereby cutting off her air supply. He could not understand why it did not fall. With tears streaming down my face, I told the doctor, "God had His thumb on that quarter!"

Mandi and I were extremely close. We did practically everything together. It broke my heart when I came home from work and discovered that she had moved out. This chapter of our lives took place in her senior year of high school, approximately three months before graduation. I cried for three solid weeks, day and night. This hurt our relationship terribly for a short season. My concern was that she was not in church. Nevertheless, I knew I raised her in the word of God, and I continued to pray for her. I was not about to give up on her or give up on God bringing her back to the place she needed to be.

Since that time, Mandi and her husband, Scott, have three children of their own. Now, she is walking with God, and they are raising their children to love and worship God with all their hearts. God has truly restored our relationship and the relationship she has with Him. To God be the glory!

Raise and nurture your children in the Lord; you may go through some very trying difficulties but, in the end, the rewards are great. "Train up a child in the way he should go, and when he is old he will not depart from it" (Proverbs 22:6, NKJV). There is no greater reward, no greater joy or greater peace for a parent, than to know his or her child is serving the Lord. It is wonderful to know they have accepted Jesus Christ, as Lord and Savior; they are filled with the Holy Spirit, and walking in God's perfect will.

In fact, my husband, Tom, and I were keeping our grandchildren this past week. The two girls, Kyra and Sierra, are seven and five, the baby boy, Zack, is only six weeks old. My daughter was having surgery, so we had the children the whole week. I was in heaven! At one point during the course of their stay with us, I missed the girls.

I went to the bedroom door to check on them and before opening the door, I heard them singing. They were singing unto the Lord with all their hearts. This is what they were singing: "Here I am to bow down, here I am to worship, here I am thanking You for saving my soul." They sang this repeatedly. Can you imagine how that touched this grandmother's heart?

Our other two grandchildren, Andrew, ten, and Hannah, seven, are also saved and filled with the Spirit. The fact that our grandchildren are taught the word of God, and brought up in the admonition of the Lord, fills our hearts with such joy and peace.

Last, but not least, we have a new grandson on the way. Stephanie and Blake are expecting their first child any time now. His name is Broxton. I am very confident that he, too, will be brought up to love and serve the Lord with all his heart.

Tom and I give glory and honor to God for the transformation He is making in our lives and the lives of all our children, their spouses, and our grandchildren. We truly have a great deal for which to be thankful. We are extremely proud of them all! Even though we have made mistakes raising our children, and they have made mistakes growing up, we know that they love the Lord! In the end, this is the relationship, which counts.

Remember, it starts with you serving the Lord. Then, when this happens, the multiplication begins. You are like a kernel of corn, planted in the earth, dying to self and living for God. When the kernel of corn is planted, the shoot appears then the stalk, then the ear of corn, and finally the kernels of corn. Can you imagine how many ears and how many kernels come from one tiny seed? Do you see the multiplication process of a godly heritage in your children, your grandchildren, and your great grandchildren? Right down to the very last generation! Are you willing to sacrifice self for a godly heritage, with the assurance of an eternity with God for you and the generations to come?

Standing on the Promises of God

My son, Jesse, is very special, because he is our only son and our namesake. He always had a very tender heart; but he tried to hide it. I guess it was his defense mechanism to avoid getting hurt. We are a lot alike in that area. In addition, because we were so much alike, we butted heads a lot! However, that did not hinder our love for each other, in the least.

Now, I brought him up in church and in the word of God. When he was sixteen years old, he started hanging around with the wrong crowd. He became involved with some things he should not have. I guess, he was going through a stage, where he thought his parents knew absolutely nothing and his so-called friends knew everything. It was not long before he realized who really cared about him and who really loved him. The problem was that it was now too late. He was in over his head. No, not even his parents could help him now. We could only relinquish him into the hands of God. He was his only hope!

He had run away from home and was staying with a person, who he thought was his friend. All of his friends were hiding him from us. I searched for him many mornings before I went to work. I searched for him during my lunch break and then again after work. At times, I was out until nine and ten o'clock, trying to find him. We just wanted him to know how much we loved him and missed him. We wanted him to come back home, where he would be safe and secure.

Finally, one day, he came out and talked with me. I could not believe how thin he had become; he looked like skin and bones. He said he had been praying and wanted to come home to get his life straightened out. He knew he had a call on his life for young people. I begged him to come home with me that day; but he had a friend coming in from out of town he wanted to see. He promised me I could come pick him up the next day. Only the next day was too late! I let my guard down; I did not continue to pray, as I had been praying. I thought everything was going to be all right. However, it was far from over and being all right!

A young man, my son and our entire family had befriended, called me and told me he had a dream or a vision about Jesse. Anthony knew Jesse was in deep trouble but did not know what the trouble was at the time. Anthony wanted to talk to Jesse, to let Jesse know he was praying for him. He also knew the call my son had on his life. This young man is now a pastor with a family of his own. I know to this very day that this young pastor is still praying for my son. I thank God for Anthony's prayers and the many others that I know are praying.

You see, my son went to prison for murder. He received a life sentence with parole at the age of seventeen. He had been seventeen for less than a week when this tragedy took place. Since he had just turned seventeen, they tried him as an adult, instead of a juvenile. He now has been in prison for almost twelve years.

Many prayers have gone up to heaven for his release. The fact is we are still waiting for those prayers to manifest. I do not know why God has not intervened in his situation. I do not know why he had to serve time in prison. I do not know why it is taking so long for God to answer our prayers; but this one thing I do know... God is in control. He knows what He is doing; He knows the plans He has for my son's life and for his ministry. Who knows what He saved him from, but God? At least we are still able to talk to him and visit him. We thank God that he is alive. *If not for God,* he could be sick, hurt, or dead.

Many parents out there are not as fortunate as we have been. For those of you that have lost your children, my heart goes out to you. It is hard enough to lose a child in a miscarriage. I cannot imagine the pain and sorrow of losing a child you loved and nurtured. I pray that God will be with you and comfort you.

Honestly, I never thought Jesse would spend one day in prison. The man Jesse hit had hit him first. If anything, it should have been self-defense. The trial took place because my son admitted to hitting the man, and the man died approximately three weeks later. The victim described to the police two large men in ski masks who had beat him with a ball bat and took his social security check. However, there was no investigation concerning his testimony of these facts; neither was there an investigation to find out who signed the social security check.

When we went to talk to the investigating officer, he told us that even though the man had been beaten and robbed on four different occasions in the span of a month's time, he did not intend to look for anyone else. He stated that his caseload was too heavy; therefore, he would not waste his time. He then stated: "Your son admitted to hitting the man, and that's all I need."

By the way, the officer was recording the conversation; but when it came time to hear the recording as evidence, conveniently, there was no such recording. His lawyer proved that the police had made four calls to the victim's house; but there was only one report written. Each time the police make a call, there is supposed to be a written report without exception. The officers supposedly made only one report. You guessed it; the only report was on our son, Jesse!

During the trial, it was also proven that the report was falsified, and the date had been changed. Not only that, but when they went to take the evidence to the jury room, the altered report was missing and had been replaced by another report. When our attorney discovered this, the judge declared a recess, stating the report had better appear by the time he came back from the recess. Sure enough, the court officials discovered the report in the investigating detective's office inside his filing cabinet, with the green evidence sticker still attached to the falsified report. The thing is that the jury did not know all this took place, because they were not in the courtroom. All the witnesses they had against my son proved to have lied on the stand during their testimony. Oddly enough, not one of the witnesses was charged with perjury! Even with all of this, the judge allowed the trial to continue.

The victim knew my son and could have identified him, if he had been the person who beat him. The man had been beaten and robbed several times; but he never mentioned my son once. Not only that, but it was stated repeatedly by the doctors, surgeons, neurologists and the coroner that Jesse could not have caused the man's death. They stated the man died from a chronic subdural hematoma.

There are three types of subdural hematomas: one shows up within days, one within weeks, and the last one is the chronic. This one shows up over a period of months after you receive a blow to the head. Therefore, Jesse could not have caused his death.

I do not understand why he and our family had to go through this, and probably never will. The point is God is bringing us through it. Day by day, with God's help, we walk it out.

In all of this, God has a way of letting us know, He is still there directing our paths, and He is still in control. For you see, the prison Jesse was in was on the same road; which led to Damascus. There was actually a road sign that stated: Damascus (so many miles). There is a town in Georgia called Damascus. This may seem far-fetched to you, but we believed this had to be a sign from God, that He was doing something mighty in his life through all of the chaos. We prayed he would have a Saul-Paul experience on the road to Damascus. We believe he will have a great anointing. It is very possible he will have a Joseph anointing, also, because he has walked through the same thing Joseph walked through. It is hard enough to pay for something you did wrong. It takes a very strong person when accused falsely to pay for a crime you did not commit, and still keep your faith. Jesse has always been a strong-willed person; this helps him to sustain his perseverance through this tremendous trial in which he is walking through, day by day. The word of God states:

> No weapon formed against you shall prosper, and every tongue
> which rises against you in judgment you shall condemn.
>
> Isaiah 54:17 (NKJV)

We also know: "If God is for us, who can be against us" (Romans 8:31, NKJV). God says:

> For your shame, ye shall have double, and for confusion, they
> shall rejoice in their portion: therefore, in their land they shall
> possess the double: everlasting joy shall be unto them.
>
> Isaiah 61.7 (KJV)

In all of this, I know that our God will take this horrible experience and turn it for good. I do not know how or when, but I know He always keeps His promises. We have been praying for a very long time and, in all honesty, sometimes we become weary. Then, I am reminded of the scripture in Isaiah:

> But they that wait upon the Lord shall renew their strength;
> they shall mount up with wings as eagles; they shall run, and
> not be weary; and they shall walk, and not faint.
>
> Isaiah 40:31 (KJV)

He is our only strength in the battle. There, again, is another promise: "For the battle is the Lord's, and He will give you (our enemies) into our hands" (1 Samuel 17:47, KJV).

I trust God will redeem the time, which has been stolen by Satan. The plan of Satan was to steal Jesse's life and his ministry. I am here to prophesy, right now, that Satan has not stolen his life or his ministry; but instead, has made it more powerful and more anointed. I prophesy he will kick down the gates of hell and receive back to himself everything that has been stolen, seven times over!

By the way, that is also his plan for you, your spouse, and your children. Do not allow Satan to steal, kill, and destroy from you and yours any longer. Take a stand; take authority, now, in the name of Jesus!

Right after, Jesse went to prison; I was very distraught, consumed by fear and anxiety. I decided to go to a women's intercessor prayer group. There was only one person there, with whom I was barely acquainted and she knew nothing about Jesse or me. When I went there that night, I just knew that I knew, God was going to show up, and show up He did! The anointing was so strong and powerful in that place. You could actually feel the anointing growing stronger and stronger. God was in the house!

All of a sudden, like the mighty rushing wind of the Holy Spirit in Acts, a lady was praying for me and she gave a message in tongues, followed by the interpretation. This message was so precious, because it was God talking just to me on behalf of my son. Can you imagine just for me? If He will do it for me, He will do it for you, too! God is no respecter of persons, according to the Word. We serve an awesome God, do you agree?

I will never forget the words, which were spoken, nor the impact it made on my life that night. It helped take away the fear and the anxiety. Little by little, the pain began to lessen. Not to say it does not hurt anymore, because it does. However, I know I serve a God Who can turn everything around. I know God protects and nurtures him. God will raise him up, just as He did with Joseph.

In my prayer time, I had prayed that God would protect him. He was the youngest inmate in the prison at that time. You hear of all the homosexual activity, the rape that goes on in prison, not to mention the AIDS epidemic. For any mother, I would think those thoughts would be horrifying! I was most fearful for Jesse for that reason. My fear was not that Jesse would participate willingly, but that it might be forced upon him.

That night at the prayer meeting, God gave me peace that passes all understanding. The message God gave me was this:

You have asked Me to send angels, to protect your son; but I tell you this: I am going Myself. I see him lying on a bed, alone and crying. I am surrounding him with fire, not a consuming fire, but a fire of protection. No harm shall come to him. I have known him from his mother's womb. I have called him by name; his name is called "Preacher." By My Word and by his testimony, many will be saved that would not ordinarily be saved. He will touch the lives of those no one else can reach.

I am still holding on to this word with all my might. I hold it close to my heart at all times; knowing in due season, He will bring it to pass.

Again, the Word says you can prophesy this over your life and the lives of your spouse, your children, and grandchildren, as well as others. Do not stand idly by, and let Satan continue to steal, kill, and destroy the people and things that are so precious to you.

Through Christ, you have the power and the anointing to stop Satan and redeem the time. Christ actually means "the anointed one" or "the anointing" Do not let Satan defeat you or yours, use the anointing you have been given. Jesus paid a great price, so that we might have the anointing of Christ. Do not cast it off, as if His death was for nothing!

We believe God, for Jesse's release every year; but he comes up for parole in 2011. I ask humbly for you to pray for him, his ministry, and our family. We are still standing on the promises of God, our Savior.

My Forgiveness

Going back in time, before all of that took place, there is another testimony I would like to share with you. It is my belief, whatever trials or tests you go through, become testimonies to help someone else through the same thing or similar circumstances. My prayer is this testimony will help others to walk through a difficult time and give them renewed hope.

Almost eight years after my son was born, I became pregnant. At two-and-a-half months into the pregnancy, I lost that child. Feelings of guilt flooded my spirit, because I had gone to an exercise class the night before. I was very upset, even though the child was unexpected.

Again, I became pregnant and carried the child for approximately two-and-a-half months; this pregnancy also ended with a miscarriage. This time it was different. My body had aborted part of the sack; therefore, I went to the hospital to have a DNC and remove the fetus (as it was referred to by the doctor). I was told a number of things which could happen to the child or me if the pregnancy was allowed to continue. Everyone was pressuring me into the abortion, because continuing the pregnancy could endanger my life. There was only a time span of approximately thirty minutes to make my decision. Reluctantly, I agreed to have the procedure.

That is when all the guilt and self-blame began to set in. I started to think, somehow, I must have caused the two miscarriages. It had to be my fault. I was not living for the Lord at that time; therefore, I thought God was punishing me. Of course, that could not have been further from the truth. I was tormenting myself! I was convinced that I murdered my two children. Yes, they were children, not just fetuses, as referred to by the doctor. I had absolutely no mercy for myself. I was far from having a clear and balanced mind. Somehow, I felt I deserved what I was doing to myself.

The guilt obsessed me, so that I even began to watch documentaries of actual abortions. This was only to serve me with more torment and self-punishment. I would sit there and watch with tears streaming down my face.

I am telling you this went on for months. I was a basket case, mentally, emotionally, and physically. My spirit, soul, and body were affected. My marriage, my children, and my home were all affected by my desire to punish myself. You talk about self-inflicted pain; I was a master at it! I cried all the time. Many nights I cried myself to sleep, only to wake up crying. My husband could not console me. It was as if I wanted to be miserable. Things had to change; but I could not change them by myself. I had to seek God's face, His love, mercy and His grace. As I said previously, I did not have mercy on myself; but I am so thankful God had all the mercy I needed. *If not for God*, I would have lost my mind.

Those of you who have had an abortion, whether it was a legal or an illegal one, whether it was for medical reasons or whatever the reason might be, God is quick to forgive. All you have to do is humble yourself before him and ask for His forgiveness. He, alone, can take away the heartache and pain you feel. He, alone, can restore your life to what He intended it to be. Then you have to forgive yourself. If God forgave you, what gives you the right not to forgive yourself?

I believe the Lord has shown me that the children who died through abortion, miscarriage, or premature death are nurtured and taught in heaven. I believe, with all my heart, when I am called home to be with the Lord, my unborn children will be there to greet me. Therefore, those of you that have lost your children, rest assured, they will be waiting for you, also. Those children are not dead, lost, or suffering. They are in the loving hands of God!

To those who are contemplating abortion for any reason, consider God's commandment first: "Thou shalt not kill." Abortion is not an option with God! Nothing is more horrific than to take an innocent life!

We have been deceived! Yes, we have been deceived by the world's standards! It is not a fetus; it is a living child, a creation of God. It is not just a glob of tissue, as some would say. It is a living being, growing inside you. Life begins at the point of conception! You cannot have growth without life. Whatever it is, if it stops growing or changing, it dies. That little life inside you grows and changes every day. Just a little fact and food for thought: did you know a baby has a heartbeat within eighteen days after conception? Life is the most precious possession we have. No child should ever be disposed of like trash!

If you are, indeed, considering abortion, allow me to challenge you to have an ultrasound test done first. After you see the miracle growing inside your body, after you get a glimpse of your baby's heartbeat; if you are still blinded, I further challenge you to sit down and watch the reality of the horrible things they do to a child who is being aborted (murdered). Please understand, no matter what they tell you, your child will feel excruciating pain. The only exception is if the baby is already dead, which means it does not have a heartbeat or brainwaves.

If you still choose not to keep your child, explore your child's options. Many couples would be ecstatic to give your child a loving home. There are numerous couples who are not able to have children of their own, but they would make wonderful parents.

If you are afraid of how your parents would react in this situation, please give them the benefit of the doubt. I have personally been through this as a parent. Honestly, it is a shock; but you are still their daughter and the child is still their grandchild. Give them a little time to get over the initial shock. More times than not, they will come through for you and the life you carry on the inside of you. Even if they do not give you the support you need, God will!

If it is the relationship you are worried about losing, then you should consider these factors: If he truly loves you, the way God intended him to love you, the way you deserve to be loved, then he will stand by you and the child. He will be a man, no matter the age, and take responsibility for you and his child. If he is not man enough to love you in this way, you are better off without him! He is not worthy of your love, and he is definitely not worth giving up your child's life!

God forgive us for sacrificing our children for convenience sake! May God be with you as you choose life or death! God is the Creator of life; only He has the right to take it!

> I call heaven and earth to record this day against you, that I have set before you life and death, blessing and cursing: therefore choose life that both thou and thy seed may live:
>
> Deuteronomy 30:19 (KJV)

If there was ever a doubt in your mind about choosing life, there is your answer. It is as plain as black and white; there is not a gray issue here! You are either for God, who chooses life, or for Satan, who chooses death. Jesus said, "I came that you will have abundant life." On the other hand, Satan came to steal, kill, and destroy. Therefore, choose you this day whom you will serve!

One day, while in the shower, and crying out to God, I literally broke down emotionally. I completely lost it! At that moment, I began to ask for His forgiveness.

I know we are not supposed to look for signs; but you will just have to forgive me. At this stage in my life, I needed to have a particular sign of forgiveness. I asked the Lord to forgive me for aborting that child. Not only that, but I asked Him to give me another child to show me He had truly forgiven me. This child would be an outward sign of the promise of my forgiveness.

God did forgive me, and He did send the child I asked of Him. Stephanie was and is the precious gift of my forgiveness, which resulted in my healing and forgiveness for me.

In fact, I wrote a poem to her on rainbow stationary. The rainbow has great significance for me and should have for you. It is God's sign to remind us of His promises. In addition, did you know in the book of Revelation, it talks about rainbows?

And He that sat there was to look upon like a jasper and a sardine stone: and there was a rainbow round about the throne, in sight like unto an emerald.

Revelation 4:3 (KJV)

Also recorded in Revelation:

And I saw another mighty angel come down from Heaven, clothed with a cloud: and a rainbow was upon his head, and his face was as it were the sun, and his feet as pillars of fire:

Revelation 10:1 (KJV)

Prophecy over me, years ago, revealed that my armor was the colors of the rainbow, which were constantly moving, teaming with life, and protecting me from the fiery darts of the enemy. I am sure you know about the "whole armor of God"; but if you do not, acquaint yourself with Ephesians 6. This is vital for your protection and for the protection of those you love. You need to apply the "whole armor of God and the rear guard, Who is the Holy Spirit" over your lives every day. My husband prays this over us every morning before we get out of bed.

Now, getting back to the poem, the title of the poem was "You Are My Forgiveness." My daughter cherished this poem so much; she shared it with a friend of hers who was unmarried and pregnant. We feel because of the love of God and the testimony of this poem, her friend decided to keep her baby. Due to God's forgiveness, a child's life was spared. We thank God for this child and the fact the mother did not have to endure the guilt I once felt.

Everything was wonderful, until I suspected I might be pregnant again. This time, I carried the child for about five-and-a-half months, only to find out the child had stopped growing three to four months into the pregnancy. The doctor ordered another DNC. This time was completely different; this time I had my relationship back with God, with Jesus, and I was full of the Holy Spirit, Who is my Comforter. You see, with these three in your life, you can face anything. I had the peace of God within my heart. No, I did not understand any of this. I probably never will. Understand this: only God can give the peace that passes all understanding. "And the peace of God, which passeth all understanding, shall keep your hearts and minds through Christ Jesus" (Philippians 4:7, KJV). He can take everything Satan meant for evil and turn it for good!

> But as for you, ye thought evil against me, but God meant it unto good to bring to pass, as it is this day, to save much people alive.
>
> Genesis 50:20 (KJV)

The thing that breaks my heart is knowing, if I had been walking with God, I might have had the faith to believe in Him to protect the children I carried before and to protect me. However, because I was not walking with God, I was walking in fear instead of in faith. Remember, if you are in fear, you are not in faith. Some time ago, I saw a message on a church sign that said, "If you pray, why worry; but if you worry, why pray?" That really stayed in my mind and in my heart all these years. If you pray and have faith, you will not worry. For if, your confidence is in the Lord, if you pray and believe, He will take care of all your concerns.

> And this is the confidence that we have in Him, that, if we ask anything according to His will, He heareth us: And if we know that He hear us, whatsoever we ask, we know that we have the petitions that we desired of Him.
>
> 1 John 5:14-15 (KJV)

If you pray and then worry, your prayer is in vain, because you are not in faith. It says in the book of Mark that if you pray and waiver not, then your prayer will be answered, and then the mountains will be moved and cast into the sea.

And Jesus answering, saith unto them, Have faith in God. For verily I say unto you, that whosoever shall say unto this mountain, Be thou removed, and be thou cast into the sea, and shall not doubt in his heart, but shall believe that those things which he saith shall come to pass: he shall have whatsoever he saith. Therefore I say unto you, What things soever ye desire, when ye pray, believe that ye receive them, and ye shall have them.

Mark 11:22-24 (KJV)

However, it also says:

But let him ask in faith, nothing wavering. For he that wavereth is like a wave of the sea driven with the wind and tossed. For let not that man think that he shall receive anything of the Lord. A double minded man is unstable in all his ways.

James 1: 6-8 (KJV)

The bottom line is it takes faith to please God and receive answers to our prayers.

But without faith it is impossible to please Him: for he that cometh to God must believe that He is, and that He is a rewarder of them that diligently seek Him.

Hebrews 11: 6 (KJV)

Faith is the evidence of things hoped for, but not seen.

Now faith is the substance of things hoped for, the evidence of things not seen. Through faith we understand that the worlds were framed by the word of God, so that things which are seen were not made of things which do appear.

Hebrews 11:1,3

In the *Layman's Bible Encyclopedia*, on page 240, it says it like this:

Faith is thought of as an act by which the individual avails himself of the gifts of God, submits himself in obedience to God's commands, and abandons all thought of self, trusting only in God. The emphasis shifts from the reliance on self to complete reliance on God. Faith is the confident trust in the unseen power of God.

Now, I like that description. In my opinion, that is a brilliant explanation. It has the power to justify; in Romans 3:28, it says we are justified by faith. It has the power to purify; in Acts 15:9, it says their hearts are purified by faith; and in Acts 26:18, we are sanctified by faith. The spirit of God gives faith and faith works through love, Who is Jesus Christ.

Faith is also part of a Christian's armor. In Ephesians, it tells us to take up the "shield of faith": "Above all, taking the shield of faith, wherewith ye shall be able to quench all the fiery darts of the wicked" (Ephesians 6:16, (KJV).

Now, you may think you have all the faith you can muster; but unless you do something to go along with it, faith will not work. Each time Jesus, the disciples, or the prophets healed someone, they told them to do something. Healing came after they did what they commanded them to do. The key word here is *after*. Absolutely nothing took place, not one thing changed, until after they did what they told them to do. You have to have obedience!

Even so faith, if it hath not works, is dead being alone. Yea, a man may say, Thou hast faith, and I have works: shew me thy faith without thy works, and I will shew thee my faith by my works. Thou believest that there is one God, thou doest well: the devils also believe, and tremble. But wilt thou know, O vain man, that faith without works is dead?

James 2:17-20 (KJV)

Do you have faith in God? Do you trust Him unconditionally? Do you love Him unconditionally? The only way you can have faith in God, love and trust in Him, is to know Him intimately. The only way you can know Him intimately is to know His Son, Jesus Christ, as your Lord and Savior, intimately. That means spending quality time with Jesus, loving on Him, sharing every part of your life with Him. As my pastor says, you cannot truly love someone until you know him or her. To the extent that you know them, the more you are able to love them.

QUESTIONS FOR REFLECTION

Have you experienced the loss of a child—whether it is through sickness, accident, miscarriage, abortion or any other tragedy?

Did you suffer any form of condemnation from yourself or from others?

Are you tormenting or punishing yourself or those around you because you are in so much pain?

Is your life consumed by this loss?

How can you go forward so you are able to lead a productive life?

Do you understand that God is merciful, and full of unmerited grace; which gives Him the power to forgive and forget if you ask Him?

Have you asked for forgiveness from God?

Have you forgiven everyone involved including yourself?

PRAYER

Father,

I ask for your forgiveness if I have caused the death of a child, knowingly or unknowingly. If it came about by deception or through any other means from others, I ask that you forgive them. Help me to forgive all who were involved including me. Change my heart and my lifestyle, so I am not faced with this again. Whether the abortion was done out of fear, ignorance or for the sake of convenience, I ask that you not only forgive me; but also take away the pain, the shame, the guilt and condemnation from my memory. Give me Your strength and power to put all my trust and faith in You, Lord. Restore my life completely. Give me wisdom to go forward and lead a godly and productive life. These things I ask in the name of Jesus. Amen.

The Greatest Miracle of All

For those of you whose lives are scarred by cancer, I say to you that Christ is the "Big C," not the disease. Every name has to bow at the name of Jesus Christ, even cancer! We find this passage in Philippians:

> Wherefore God also hath highly exalted Him, and given Him a name which is above every name: That at the name of Jesus every knee should bow, of things in heaven, and things in earth, and things under the earth; And that every tongue should confess that Jesus Christ is Lord, to the glory of God the Father.
>
> Philippians 2:9-11 (KJV)

That means every sickness, every disease, every infirmity, and every circumstance, even poverty. There are no exceptions to this rule!

My daddy suffered with cancer for approximately seven years. At the time, he was not saved. Growing up as a little girl, I always tried to be the peacemaker of the family. As far back as I can remember, I still vividly remember praying for Daddy to receive his salvation.

Please, do not get me wrong, Daddy loved his family very much; but he had a drinking problem, and it caused great sorrow to our family. Mother and Daddy loved each other very much; but the severity of the drinking caused a lot of discord in our home.

Many years passed; then when Daddy was in his early fifties, he was diagnosed with lung cancer. This journey was hard on all involved. It was extremely hard on him, but also just as hard on Mother, if not harder. Several times, we received calls from the hospital with the words: "It could be any time now." Somehow, he kept hanging on, and he would always pull out of it.

On one occasion, Daddy was supposed to have surgery to have a large portion of his lung removed. I went to the prayer room in the hospital to pray, because I did not have peace about the surgery. I prayed, "God, if this is not your will for him to have the surgery, then please do not let them operate." Do you want to know how amazing God is? They could not find his chart; therefore, they could not operate.

Again, they scheduled the surgery to remove the cancer, and again I went to the prayer room and prayed the exact same prayer. "Father, if it is not Your will for him to have this surgery, please do not allow them to operate." This time they proceeded with trying to put him to sleep for the surgery, but he had trouble breathing. They immediately brought him out of the anesthesia and never attempted to do the surgery again. We may not know the outcome; but God knows all things, from beginning to end. It was not his time to go!

I continued to pray for his salvation. Daddy became extremely ill again; they had to rush him back to the VA Hospital. The hospital was over a hundred miles away. Mother was staying with him at the hospital, sleeping in a foldout chair. She did this for several weeks, and it was really taking a toll on her. The family drove back and forth, three and four times a week.

Remembering back, I would drive down there after work, stay the night with Daddy, and then leave about four thirty in the morning. I arrived home in time to get the children to school and me to work. My husband kept them for me while I ran back and forth to the hospital.

During this stay, they called us again saying, "This is it, you better come now!" This time the whole family went, praying all the way down there. Afraid we would not make it in time; I kept praying and reading Scripture. I began reminding God that I had prayed ever since I could remember that Daddy would receive salvation. I kept saying, "You cannot let Satan have him. You said if I was saved, You would save my household." I did not believe Daddy was ready to meet God at that moment, and I knew the consequences.

When we walked into the room, he was so frail and pale. His body seemed lifeless. The doctors were telling us we needed to say our good-byes. They did not know how he could make it through the night. You could just feel death all around him. I knew I had to be alone with God. I was not going to give up without a fight.

Alone with God, I began to intercede for Daddy, for his spirit man. I knew this was the turning point for him; it was heaven of hell! His time was running out to make his choice between heaven and hell! Crying out to God, I pleaded with Him to show me something I could do to stop the death angel from taking him before he was ready.

All of a sudden, it was as if I caught a glimpse in time of Moses and the death angel. Do you remember the story in the Bible about the angel of death coming for the entire first born? Many people have the misconception that the Lord caused their death; but they caused this curse to come upon themselves. The Lord protected those covered under the blood. He passed (covered) over the doors, which had the blood of the lamb. The Lord's covering prevented the destroyer or the death angel from entering.

> For the Lord will pass through to smite the Egyptians; and when He seeth the blood upon the lintel, and on the two side posts, the Lord will pass over the door, and will not suffer (allow or permit) the destroyer to come unto your houses to smite you.
>
> Exodus 12:23 (KJV)

He had done this same thing with Moses when Moses was in the cleft of the Rock. God protected Moses by covering him. In other words, He protects the righteous; but we still have the responsibility to be in obedience for, you see, even though they were righteous, they had to cover their doorposts with the blood of the lamb. The blood represented the blood of Jesus Christ. If they had not been obedient, the first-born of every person and every animal would have been destroyed, along with the unrighteous. We all have an appointed time to die; but this prevents the enemy from taking us before our time.

The unrighteous did not have the protection of the Lord; therefore, the destroyer was allowed to enter. As a result, the entire first born died. Of course, the lamb's blood symbolizes the blood of Jesus Christ. The doorposts are representations of our lives. Unless the blood covers our lives, we are doomed to an eternity of torment and damnation! Are you covered by the blood of the Lamb, Who is Jesus Christ?

Suddenly, a peace came over me; I cannot explain. You know, the peace that passes all understanding! I just knew what the Lord was prompting me to do. Some of you may think, "*I know this lady has completely lost it! She must be some kind of fruit loop!*" I probably would have thought the same thing, if I had not known the voice of God.

Immediately, I stood up, stopped crying, and went directly to Daddy's room. The death spirit was so strong; you could actually feel the presence of death all around, not only in his room, but also outside his door in the hallway. I suspect that most people would refer to the spirit of death as a thing; but this was more like a person or a being, instead. It was as if you could actually reach out and touch him!

Our family was getting ready to go back to the hotel for the night. I asked them to wait for me, because I had to do what God showed me before I left. I know this sounds crazy; but I went in his room, prayed over him, and covered him with the blood of Jesus. The best way I know how to describe what happened next is this: In my mind's eye, I took a paintbrush and started applying the "Blood of Jesus" over my daddy's whole body. I mean from head to toe. Next, I went to his window and covered the top and the sides, just like they did the doorposts. I went to Daddy's bedside and proceeded to do the same thing, covering him and his bed with the "Blood of Jesus," visually. I told him I loved him, kissed him, and told him I would see him in the morning. As I walked out the door of the room, I did the same thing over the doorposts. Standing outside the door, I prayed: "Father, you said, whatever was bound on earth was bound in heaven, and whatever was loosed on earth was loosed in heaven. Now, Father, I bind the death angel's hands, in the name of Jesus. I bind them, so they cannot take him before he is saved." As soon as I prayed that prayer, I felt that spirit leave. I am talking instantly! Great peace filled that place. I knew he was going to be there in the morning. Not only that, but I knew in my heart, he would, in fact, be saved.

Early the next morning, I called the hospital and spoke to the nurse in his room. She told me she really did not expect to find him there that morning. She stated that he made a remarkable turn around and was eating breakfast, which he had not been able to do. He made the comment to her that he was starving.

Daddy did extremely well for about six months, and then started getting sicker. We took him back to the hospital. During this stay, a pastor from his hometown stopped in to see him. His made his peace with God and now was ready to go to his eternal home. In my heart, I feel he was just holding on for his sixtieth birthday, which was also Mother and Daddy's wedding anniversary. Please understand, it was not that Jesus could not heal him; however, it is my belief he was just plain tired of fighting, therefore he gave up. He just wanted to go to his heavenly home.

I spoke with my pastor and told him the whole story concerning the death angel and what the Lord instructed me to do. He knew Daddy was barely holding on and suffering tremendously. One day he spoke with me and reminded me of the scripture I prayed about binding and loosing on earth and in heaven. My pastor helped me realize that since I had bound the death angel's hands, they would have to be loosed, in order, for Daddy to be released. Believe me; that was the hardest thing I have ever had to do! Not wanting to let go, but knowing he would not suffer any longer, he would finally be safe in the "arms of God." Only through God was I able to find the strength to release him.

Approximately two weeks later, Daddy went to be with the Lord. Ironically, the same pastor who prayed with him earlier just happened to be there. Daddy had his hand on the Bible we gave him for his birthday. He heard the pastor talking in the next room and asked my brother to go get him so the pastor could pray with him. The pastor came in, took him by the hand, and prayed with him, as the family gathered around. Regrettably, I was unable to be there to participate in his home going. They told me that as the pastor prayed, Daddy looked up toward the ceiling and began to radiate the biggest smile ever. When the pastor finished his prayer, Daddy drew his last breath here on earth and his first breath in heaven!

I thank Jesus for saving Daddy's soul. I thank Him for His faithfulness. *If not for God*, he would not be in heaven today. I know I will see him again one day, one day soon! I am eternally grateful that God is faithful and true. He keeps His promises, yes, every one of them!

Through this situation with my Daddy, God gave me the revelation of the power and authority we have, as Christians. We have the power and authority to bind and loose, even if it is death you are facing. Yes, we have power over death, hell and the grave because of Jesus Christ! We can bind the death angel's hands and we can loose abundant life into lives and situations. Of course, you must realize that if the Lord is calling a person home, His will prevails!

> I tell you this: Whatever you prohibit (bind) on Earth is prohibited (bound) in Heaven and whatever you allow (loose) on Earth is allowed (loosed) in Heaven.
> Matthew 18:18 (NLT)

Many times the Lord brought this particular prayer back to my memory, and many times, I have prayed in the same manner for others and myself. This prayer was not used just for the sick, but for those who were in tragic accidents. People who, by all the standards of medical knowledge, could not have survived or would have been severely brain damaged. The thing is that the Holy Spirit only allowed me to pray that particular prayer for certain ones. This prayer consisted of binding the death angel's hands, or the spirit of death and all the effects, along with covering them with the blood of Jesus, the name of Jesus, the Word, and loosing life into them: spirit, soul, and body. A word of wisdom, if you are ever prompted by the Spirit of God to pray in this manner, make sure you cover yourself with the "whole armor of God," by the Word, Jesus Christ, by His blood, and His name, before you proceed!

QUESTIONS FOR REFLECTION

Are you aware of the arsenal of weapons you have as a Christian through Christ Jesus, such as the whole armor of God, the Word, the blood of Jesus, the name of Jesus, prayer and fasting?

Do you apply these weapons to your life daily?

What areas of your life, such as death, sickness, poverty, addiction, or ungodly relationships do you need to bind up and cast out?

In what areas do you need salvation, healing, deliverance, protection, and/or provision released into your life?

Have you used the strategy of binding and loosing in your prayer life?

If you have not, will you now use the power and authority you have through binding and loosing in heaven and on earth?

PRAYER

Father,

I ask the Holy Spirit to teach me about the weapons of warfare. Give me clear understanding on how, when and where they are to be implemented. Remind me to put on the "whole armor of God" everyday. I thank You, that the Holy Spirit is my Rearguard, according to Isaiah 58:8. Help me to saturate myself with the Word of God. Jesus, cover my loved ones and me with Your precious blood and Your name. Instruct me concerning the power and authority I have through binding and loosing. You said in the Lord's Prayer, "Thy kingdom come, Thy will be done on earth as it is in heaven." Therefore, give me the revelation that anything, which is in heaven, can be released or loosed into my life here on earth. Furthermore, reveal that anything, which is not in heaven, I have the power and authority to bind it up so it cannot harm my loved ones or me. I thank You, Lord, for the wisdom, knowledge, understanding and revelation concerning these principles. In the name of Jesus, I pray. Amen.

The Great Physician

During the time all this was taking place with Daddy, a large lump appeared on one of my breasts. Sharp pains would shoot through my breast area. It was like a hard mass. Some of you, I am sure, can imagine the fear that gripped me, especially with everything else that was happening. Remember what Job said:

> For the thing which I greatly feared is come upon me, and that which I was afraid of is come unto me.
>
> Job 3:25 (KJV)

For approximately three months, I kept this to myself. Finally, I confided in my sister-in-law, Terry, vowing her to secrecy. She urged me to go to the doctor. Fearful of what the outcome would be, I could not force myself to make an appointment. My mind was already made up that if this should be my fate, I would not have the surgery or any type of treatment. After observing everything my daddy went through, I did not think I could bear it.

One Sunday during a church service, the pastor called me up front and stated he felt impressed to pray for me. Next, he called one of the ladies in the church to come stand with me. He then asked the woman to turn facing me, and requested she lay her hand on my chest. He said the Lord said, "The thing you have feared most has come upon you." I burst out into tears. Then the Lord said, "Do not fear, because as of tonight you are healed."

The mass did not go away instantly, nor did the pain stop right at that moment. I kept speaking the word of God, words of healing.

The next thing I knew, the pain had stopped shooting through my chest, and the hard mass was gone. Hallelujah! Thank You, Jesus!

If not for God, there is no telling what would have become of me. Sometimes healing happens instantly; sometimes, in order for it to manifest, it takes your spoken words, united with the spoken word of God. Remember this: Christ is the "Big C," not cancer!

Do not deceive yourself; fear can do exactly what the Word says it can. In addition, anxiety will cause you to begin to think and say negative things over yourself.

The Word says, "For as he thinketh in his heart, so is he" (Proverbs 23:7, KJV). Be careful of the things you think and say. Purpose your thoughts and your speech to line up with the word of God.

In Mark 11:23, it says (paraphrasing), "See the mountain, speak to it and it will move; if you believe what you say; then you can have what you said." Your words have power and influence over your life and those around you, even situations and circumstances. Your thoughts become your words. Be careful what you speak; you may just get it! It does not matter, whether it is good or evil, it will come to pass. It is what you think and speak that count. What you think and say is what you create! So, what are you creating? Are you creating positive or negative things in your life?

This is a law, which is not contingent on whether you believe it, or not. This law was set in force from the beginning of time and will be in effect for eternity. God set it in motion in Genesis, when He spoke everything into existence. We are speaking spirits! What are you speaking? Are you speaking life or death, blessing or cursing? Ask yourself, *What is in my heart?* In the book of Luke, it states:

A good man out of the good treasure of his heart bringeth forth that which is good, and an evil man out of the evil treasure of his heart bringeth forth that which is evil; for out of the abundance of the heart his mouth speaketh.

Luke 6:45 (KJV)

QUESTIONS FOR REFLECTION

Are you speaking life or death into your life?

Are you praying God's Word over yourself, your loved ones and all situations or circumstances?

Does fear consume you in any area?

Whose report will you believe?

PRAYER

Father,

Replace my fear with faith for You have not given me a spirit of fear. Give me a supernatural anointing of faith so I may trust in You more. Give me the words to speak when I find myself or a loved one in a difficult situation, knowing through Your words, I will not make matters worse,but I will make them better. Show me the scriptures I need to pray for every situation or circumstance, so that I may agree with Your Word. You and I are agreeing together, and You said where two agree as touching anything it shall be done. I believe Your Word is true. I pray that I will not mumble or complain; but instead I will praise and worship You for I know my help comes from the Lord. I will believe the report of the Lord! Amen

Miracle of Obedience

"Obedience is better than sacrifice," according to God's Word.

> But Samuel replied, "What is more pleasing to the LORD; your burnt offerings and sacrifices or your obedience to His voice? Obedience is far better than sacrifice."
>
> 1 Samuel 15:22 (NLT)

Miracles come through obedience. I am reminded of the story in 1 Kings 17, where it tells us about the widow woman and the Prophet Elijah. She and her son were literally starving to death because there was a famine in the land. Do you remember the story? The widow had just enough flour and oil to make a cake of bread. She had already made plans for her and her son to give up and die. When you give up, it not only affects you, but it affects those around you, as well.

The Prophet Elijah arrived just in time, as God commanded. The Lord had already prepared the widow's heart to receive the prophet. She might not have been obedient to the voice of the prophet, if the Lord had not spoken to her before the prophet arrived. Due to her obedience in giving the prophet a cup of water and making him a cake first, God met the needs of the widow woman and her son. They did not have to die, and they were not without provision ever again. Not only that, but the prophets needs were met as well. The Word declares that if we receive a prophet, we will receive the prophet's reward. As the result of her obedience, the widow was able to save the lives of both she and her son. In addition, she was able to restore provision back to their home. Now that is awesome!

> For thus says the LORD God of Israel: "The bin of flour shall not be used up, nor shall the jar of oil run dry, until the day the LORD sends rain on the earth."
>
> 1 Kings17:14(NKJV)

The miracle I would like to share with you came about through obedience in giving and adhering to the voice of God. Three weeks to the day, (twenty-one days), before the miracle, my children and I were in church, as we were usually every time the doors were open. This particular day, I was in the church nursery upstairs; my children were sitting with some friends. In the nursery, we were fortunate enough to have a sound system and a large picture window, which allowed us to observe, what was taking place in the service.

During the service, they proceeded to take up an offering for a special need. The Lord spoke to my heart to give; but I did not have any cash with me. The only check I brought was my tithe check. I did not know what to do; but I knew God spoke to me to give. I asked the Lord to make a way. All of a sudden, the pastor said, "If there is someone here that would like to give, but does not have the means to give at this moment, I have twenty dollars in my coat pocket." I knew that was my answer!

I began waving my hands frantically in the large window in the nursery. I finally managed to get the pastor's attention, letting him know I wanted to give the twenty dollars. Everybody started lining up in the prayer line to give his or her offering. My son, Jesse, received the twenty dollars from the pastor and took his place in the prayer line, along with his friend, Ruben, who also took an offering on behalf of his family. In the midst of the prayer over the offering, a special message was given in tongues, and then the interpretation. The message was this, "For those of you who were obedient in giving, there will be special miracles. Some miracles will come within seven days, some will come within fourteen days, and some will come within twenty-one days."

That excited me and gave me great expectations of what was to come. You see, I had been praying for a car. Some of you probably know what I mean when I say, "It was on its last leg." I just knew, without any doubt, this was going to be my miracle. The anticipation was so great; I could hardly wait for the twenty-one days to be over. Little did I know what the future had in store!

Seven days drug by, and still nothing, to show for the miracle I was expecting. Fourteen days went by, and still nothing. There were miracles taking place in peoples' lives all over the church.

On Friday, which was the nineteenth day, my children, one of their friends, and I were in the middle of town when my car stalled on a railroad track. The transmission stopped working in forward gear. In other words, it would only go in reverse. We had to get out and push it out of the road. We were all so embarrassed. When I got over the embarrassment and the anger of being left on the side of the road, I thought this is it, now; I will have to get a new car. After all, I had to have a way to get back and forth to work. All day Saturday, I expected a car to appear out of the clear, blue sky; but that did not happen.

Some friends of ours came over for supper on that Saturday night. This couple and their two children were in the church where my children and I attended. The couple was also my youngest daughter's Godparents. When they started to leave, they asked if the children could spend the night with them. My daughter, Mandi, was ten years old, my son, Jesse, was eight, and Stephanie was only fifteen months old. Ladies, I am sure you will understand! We decided to allow the two older children to go, but was not comfortable with letting the "baby" go.

On Sunday morning, I was surely wondering and asking God all sorts of questions, like, "*God, did I miss it? Did I misunderstand what You said? What did I do to stop the miracle, which was prophesied? If that was not my miracle, then, God, what could it be?*" All the while, thinking, well, today is the twenty-first day. God is never too late; God is always on time. I still, had my misguided hope for that new car.

That morning, Stephanie, Cyndi, a friend of Mandi's, and I went to church. We arrived at church a little late. I noticed my friend's vehicle was not at church, which was very strange to me, because she was usually early. Making the statement to Cyndi that I wondered where Rosa could be, I noticed a woman in the churchyard. Not knowing, of course, that my children had spent the night with Joe and Rosa, the woman came over and asked me to pray, because Rosa and her children, Rachel and Ruben, had been in an accident. My heart began pounding uncontrollably with fear. The first words out of my mouth were, "Oh my God, my children are with Rosa!"

I can remember the panic so clearly, even now, to the point that it brings tears to my eyes.

Questioning the woman, I was asking were they okay, where did it happen, and where are they now? She explained all she knew was the church had received a phone call from Rosa's mother-in-law, screaming with panic in English and in Spanish. All they understood was that there had been an accident, Ruben's head was split, severely, and he was pouring blood.

This young boy, Ruben, was approximately seven years old. Only by God's grace, His mercy, and His strength could he have made it to his grandmother's house. He had to run down the road, up an embankment, across an overpass (which is extremely busy with traffic), and down the other side of the embankment to get to his grandmother.

When they received the call, the pastor and Joe (Rosa's husband) headed out to find where the accident had taken place. They called an ambulance on the way there. They actually found them before the ambulance arrived; but the church did not know they had found them. Cyndi's mother, Ann, worked at the hospital in the emergency room. I called her to see if she had heard anything about the accident. The only thing she knew was there were two ambulances with five passengers on the way to the hospital. She did not know of their condition.

The pastor drove up as I was preparing to go to the hospital. He was on one side of the street, and I was on the other. It was as though I was frozen in time. I was petrified of what I was about to hear. He just stood there, as if he did not know what to say. Finally, we both took a step forward from what seemed like an eternity. The first thing he said to me was, "You got your miracle!" Nothing, I mean nothing, else mattered, especially not material things. God had protected my children! Not only did He give me my miracle; He gave me two! The most precious miracles He could have given me were my children! God always comes through with His nature of "exceedingly, abundantly more." Remember, this was the twenty-first day after the obedience, after the prophecy, and after the giving.

As the pastor went into the church to call everyone to intercession on our behalf, the pastor's wife drove us to the hospital. I just remember praying in tongues all the way to the hospital. It seemed like it took us forever to get there, even though we were only a few blocks from the hospital. Then we had to wait for the ambulance to get there with their precious cargo. Someone from the church went to pick up my husband, because he did not attend church with us.

That day was one of those great and terrible days of the Lord! God had kept His Word! God had intervened in what could have been every parent's worst nightmare! They were all severely injured. My friend, Rosa, had injuries to her neck and back, if I remember correctly. She also had broken ribs and a punctured lung. She had tubes running in and out of her. Rosa's daughter, Rachel, was about fourteen; she had injuries to her neck and back. She also had a concussion so bad, she could not see for several hours. Rosa's son Ruben's head was split wide open, because the impact caused him to go through the windshield.

My daughter, Mandi, was unconscious and crumpled in the roof of the car when they found her. The car had flipped upside down and slammed into a tree. She was not moving; naturally, the EMTs believed the worst. After reaching the hospital, she was still unconscious. They had to cut her dress off of her, for fear of moving her. We found out later she had a fractured skull and a broken collarbone. She was in a comatose state for three days. The doctors wanted to move her to another hospital, where they were equipped better and had more experience with brain injuries. They were afraid the brain would start to swell, and we would lose her. Thank God, the brain never swelled, and she soon regained consciousness. Little by little, she started to get better.

My son, Jesse, suffered from bruises, a broken collarbone, and blood in his urine. He and Ruben bounced back quickly. Boys will be boys! They were racing up and down the hallways in their wheel-chairs. They were the first of our friends and family released from the hospital with a clean bill of health. Rosa, Rachel, and Mandi would have to have a bit more time to recover.

I thank my God in heaven for Jesus Christ. I thank Jesus Christ, who endured the stripes from the beatings, for our healing. Finally, I thank the Holy Spirit, who spoke to our spirits to give out of an obedient heart. I shudder to think what would have happened to Rosa, Rachel, Ruben, Mandi, and Jesse if our families had not been obedient to the voice of the Holy Spirit.

What Joe and Rosa gave in that special offering that day, I have not a clue. It does not matter the size of the offering or the sacrifice. The obedience of the heart and the action taken are what matter. You choose to be obedient, or you choose to be disobedient; there is no in-between. You cannot buy a miracle from God; but, in your obedience, He provides your miracle, and it is always just in time!

Is it not funny, how quickly our priorities change? The things we thought were so important now seem so insignificant. God has a way of showing us the real treasures of life and love. How quickly it could all vanish. Now, do not go where I am not going! Absolutely, under no circumstance, am I saying that God caused this to happen. What I am saying is that God takes the situations and circumstances that Satan meant for evil and brings out the goodness of God's love, mercy, and His grace.

Later, we took a ride called reality, to see the car in which they had the accident. Everyone who saw the car said it was unbelievable that anyone could live through such an impact. *If not for God* being true to His Word, we would have lost five precious loved ones on that day. Now, that is an abundance of wonderful miracles!

You know, the whole time my children and friends were in the hospital, I do not think a new car crossed my mind. No, not once! However, God did provide a car later on down the road, even though it was no longer a priority. God is good all the time!

QUESTIONS FOR REFLECTION

Are you obedient to God's Word and to His voice?

Do you give, even when, it is inconvenient or when it hurts to give?

Do you have faith that God will rescue you in your time of need?

Have you come to the realization that God is never late; He is always on time?

PRAYER

Father,
I pray that I will know Your voice, like no other. I will be sensitive to Your voice and the moving of the Holy Spirit upon my life. Help me to be willing, able and obedient in all you ask me to do. I will do my best to give, even when, it is inconvenient or when it hurts. I trust You to know what I need before I need it. Prepare me for future trials and tests. Turn everything the enemy means for harm into good. I know You are ever-present in my life. You will not forsake me, and You will always be there on time to rescue me. Amen.

A Ride to Remember

This all started when my daughter, Stephanie, and I planned to go see my son, Jesse, who was now in prison. I would say Stephanie was about eleven or twelve at the time. I had been divorced for approximately a year and half. The point is that the only one I could depend on was God.

I lost my job, due to the fact I had dated the boss for several months; but now, he had someone else in his life. His girlfriend did not want me working there anymore; therefore, I lost my job. Now, I was upset for quite a while, because I felt I had been betrayed. In fact, he let me go and hired me back the next day. It is kind of a blur, now, but it was either the same day, he hired me back, or the day after that when he let me go again! How would that make you feel? After all, I had a child to support. At this time, I would like to add, that forgiveness came in this situation, also. It was years later, but God has a way of exposing you to situations so that forgiveness and healing can come. He and his girlfriend, who was now his wife, started attending the same church that I attended. I was now married and I had moved approximately twenty-five miles away. His wife and I became friends and actually ministered healing to each other. For this, I am grateful to God for He is faithful!

Talk about a chain reaction; here is one for you. Before I could find another job, they repossessed my car. After that, my brother gave me a car, which was not the best in the world, but it did get me where I needed to go. It was one of those that your child says, "Just let me out here, I'll walk the rest of the way." I was thankful to my brother for coming to my rescue, and for the car; but lo and behold, the motor blew up in it.

As I mentioned, we were planning to take a trip to go see Jesse. He was about one hundred and fifty miles away from where we lived. A friend of mine decided to loan me her car on Friday, so I could go see him on Saturday. We had planned to leave about six thirty, Saturday morning. When we went to get in the car, we noticed the passenger door was open and so was the glove compartment. Someone had broken into the car, and had stolen her stereo and her cassette tapes. I did not take time to call the police, because we had a limited period in which to get there and visit with Jesse. Therefore, we decided to go on and fill out a report when we got back.

If that was not enough, about halfway up there, I realized the brakes were not working. I rolled into the repair shop to find out why I did not have brakes. One of the brake pads had fallen completely off the car! Now, I was thinking, *God, You are going to have to do something here, because there is no telling how much this repair bill is going to cost.* Keep in mind, I only had thirty-five dollars to my name and was out of a job. I was honest with the man and told him the amount I had with me. Thank God, they repaired the brakes and only charged me twenty-five dollars. This left ten dollars to buy food for all three of us that day.

We had a good visit with Jesse, and then we headed home. We wanted to get home before dark, which would have been about five-thirty, because it was wintertime. Everything was going perfectly fine. Stephanie and I were enjoying each other's company, talking, and having a great time; when all of sudden, the car started losing power. It left us stranded out in the middle of nowhere. Back then, I could not call on anyone, except God. That was back before the age of seven and eight year olds having cell phones.

We got out and walked to a house, which was not too far away; only, no one was home. I began to pray; I was getting frantic and desperate. Here we were, approximately one hundred miles from home; it was getting very cold, and the sun was starting to set. There we were, two females, out in the middle of no man's land, hungry, tired, and, to say the least, extremely frustrated. I remember saying to the Lord, "Lord, I don't care what you have to do; if you have to send a host of angels to help us, please do it!"

Suddenly, a woman pulled up behind us. I saw this car pass by earlier, but it did not stop. You could tell she was very hesitant about stopping. I found out in our conversation that she was a Church of God pastor's wife. She had gotten almost to the next town when the Lord spoke to her and told her to go back and help us. God is so amazing! She offered to let us use her cell phone to call someone to come rescue us. One would think this story would have ended here, not so. Evidently, that was not God's plan. You would know; we could not reach a soul on the phone.

What happened next, if I did not know this to be the truth and had experienced it myself, I would not believe it? We were sitting in the woman's car when, all of sudden, Stephanie said she smelled smoke. Sure enough, we looked back to find there were flames and smoke boiling out from under the woman's car. She grabbed her cell phone and purse; we jumped out and ran to get away from the car, not knowing if it would blow up or not.

If you do not believe God has a sense of humor, listen to this: she was calling the operator in order to get in touch with the fire department when, unexpectedly, marching down the road, we see a parade! I kid you not! Now, I am talking floats, clowns, music, police officers, and behind it a fire truck.

They put the fire out, first, and then told us the catalytic converter heated up the dead grass underneath the car and started the fire. We were very blessed because it was right where the gas tank was located. The woman called her husband, explained everything to him, and asked him to meet us. The pastor and another man towed the car back to the police/fire department. Still, we were unable to find anyone at home to come pick us up. This couple was so kind. They stayed with us, and even offered for us to spend the night at their home. The pastor spoke with the police to try to arrange for us to get back home. I wish I could remember the couples' name so I could thank them properly; but I was so stressed that day, I was doing well to remember my own name! If you should happen to read this, I would personally like to thank you for your obedience to the voice of God and for your help. It was very much appreciated!

You will never guess how we made it home. We had never been in a law enforcement car until that day. It truly was a ride to remember! The sheriff's department transported us from county line to county line, all the way home. Looking back, it is hilarious now; but it definitely was not then. It took twelve cars to get us to our destination. Trust me; it was enough to last a lifetime!

If not for God speaking to those along our pathways, arranging big and little things, where would we be today? Maybe God has arranged a parade just for you! Remember, answers to prayers do not always look like what we think they should!

QUESTIONS FOR REFLECTION

I am sure you have had days like this, when everything that could go wrong did. My question to you is did you respond in a positive manner or a negative one?

Did you pray about it right away or did you pray as a last resort?

Who did you trust, God or man, to rescue you from your situation?

In retrospect, can you laugh about it now or does it bring back bad memories?

Do you believe God has a sense of humor?

PRAYER

Father,

When things go wrong in my life, help me to respond in a positive manner. Instead of loosing my dignity and self-control, give me peace in every situation. Remind me to take the time to pray, first. Help me to put my trust in You more than man. Give me joy so I may laugh at the enemy and the tactics he uses to try to distract me. The things Satan meant for evil, You will turn them for good. You are always in control and nothing that happens to me catches You off guard. You have me in the palm of Your hand. Amen.

Christmas of Miracles

Keep in mind the episode of the broken down car that I borrowed from a friend, the stolen stereo, and tapes. My friend was very upset with the fact I had to leave her car in another town, not to mention the stereo and tapes, which were stolen. Of course, they wanted everything fixed and replaced, which I fully understood. Also, keep in mind I was unemployed, broke, and it was quickly approaching Christmas.

Now, here I was financially distraught, no income, with three children to buy Christmas for, and not the first Christmas present had been purchased. My two oldest children did not live with me at the time; but, like any mother, I wanted to be able to give them something for Christmas. Thank God, about two weeks before Christmas, He provided a position at the local hospital. The problem was that I would not draw a paycheck until one week after Christmas. God also provided, through some church family, a vehicle to get back and forth to work and to take my daughter to school. They were so gracious in their giving in every area. They told me I could have it as long as I needed it. Finally, there seemed to be a light at the end of this long, dark, winding tunnel.

Stephanie had to sleep with me, because we did not have a bed for her. She was at an age where she wanted a bedroom of her own. The thing I wanted most to get her for Christmas was a bedroom suite. However, at the same time, I was thinking, *You cannot even afford a bed, much less a bedroom suite.* Little did I know, Stephanie was praying for a bedroom suite for Christmas, as well as a CD player. In the natural realm this was impossible; but not in the spiritual!

I have not forgotten, and I pray I never forget the awesomeness of God. The Sunday morning before Christmas Day, which was the following Tuesday, God again showed Himself strong. He illuminated to us, the unlimited power of His love, mercy and grace, which He bestows upon us, as His children.

That Sunday morning did not start out with the hope of a miracle in the making. We got up and dressed for church that morning, only to find out the car would not start. I called the church to get someone to come pick us up.

In fact, we did arrive at church in time for Sunday school. Would you believe our lesson was on being thankful? The teacher asked each of us to recall the best Christmas that we could remember. All the while, it was getting closer and closer to my turn. The closer it got, the more I thought to myself, "*Well, it sure isn't this Christmas!*" Instead of focusing on the "reason for the season," Jesus Christ, I focused on my situation, my circumstances, and myself. My entire focus was on my lack, instead of my provider, Jehovah-Jireh.

When my turn came, I blurted out just what I was thinking, "Well, it sure isn't this Christmas!" Immediately, I was so ashamed, and I heard the Lord rebuke me, saying, "Take it back; this may be your best Christmas, ever." It took me a few minutes to get over the embarrassment I brought upon myself, and to get over the shock of hearing the rebuke of the Spirit of God. I repeatedly heard the Spirit saying, "Take it back, take it back." At that moment, I knew I had to make things right! Finally, I gathered up enough courage to ask for everyone's attention. I asked the class to forgive me, and I asked for God's forgiveness. Afterwards, the sweet peace of the Holy Spirit flooded my being.

Our church was taking up a special offering that morning for one of our members, who was also an evangelist. He was preparing to go on a mission trip. I heard the Lord speak to me, in a still, soft voice, in the morning service about giving in the offering. I hate to admit it, but I argued with the Lord (I am sure you have never done that). Plain as day, I heard the Spirit say to give five dollars in the offering. I was sitting there telling the Lord, "Now Lord, You know, I only have six dollars to my name, it's two days before Christmas, and it will be another week after Christmas before I will get my first paycheck."

First, God is all-knowing; He knows not only the beginning and the end, but He knows all the in-betweens, too. Absolutely nothing catches God off guard or by surprise. You see, He knew to the penny how much money I had; He knew down to the very least and minuscule detail of what was going on around me, and He knew down to the very second when I would receive my paycheck. Secondly, the Spirit of the Lord just told me this could be the very best Christmas, ever. Thirdly, it plainly tells us in the Word, if He tells us to give and we are obedient, we will receive His blessing. I, of all people, should have recognized when God was trying to give me an abundant harvest for just a small seed. Besides, what on earth was I going to purchase with six measly dollars?

Again, the Spirit prompted me to give five dollars, of the six dollars I had. As the offering plate reached me, I quickly threw it into the offering plate, so that I could not change my mind. Somehow, I knew I had to be obedient to the voice of God. When I gave, I suddenly had a sweet peace come over my spirit once again. I just knew God was working on my behalf. God is a miracle working God; He is the Waymaker; I knew that He was working a miracle just for us!

Immediately after service, Stephanie and I received an invitation to eat with some friends, as a blessing to us. In other words, they offered to pay for our dinner. The friends who invited us to dinner were the evangelist and his wife. They were the ones who received the special offering. In addition, when they hugged our necks and shook our hands, they placed a hundred dollar bill in my hand. How is that for a quick return on seed planted? Little did we know that was only the beginning of the harvest we would receive on the obedience of a five-dollar bill. That is so like God, I gave five dollars to the evangelist in an offering, and he gave me one hundred dollars, as a love offering; not to mention buying our dinner. God is awesome! As I said before, it is not the amount of the sacrifice; but it is through our obedience that God blesses us.

After dinner, several of the church members were going to different homes where there were financial needs. They actually had boxes of money wrapped up in Christmas paper to take to the families. I went with them to distribute these gift boxes full of money. I am ashamed to say it, but I was praying I would be one the fortunate receivers of one of the boxes. To my disappointment, I was not, although I was very happy and joyful for the others who did receive their blessing. You know, God does not always do things the way we think He should!

After all the festivities were over, one of the ladies brought me home. We were just sitting there, talking about the different events, which had taken place throughout the day. Suddenly, I noticed a large truck pull into my driveway. A young man and a friend stepped out of the truck. That young man was Ruben, the boy that was in the accident with my children years earlier. He asked me if I had gotten a bed for Stephanie. I told him I had not. Then he proceeded to tell me that his sister, Rachel, was moving and wanted Stephanie to have her extra bedroom suite. What God was doing was completely overwhelming to me. Two days before Christmas, God had miraculously provided a bedroom suite, which was nearly new. Not only that, but she also gave her the pillows, bedspread, bed skirt, pillow shams, and curtains to match! Do you remember our prayers? My daughter had prayed for a bedroom suite of her own, and I had prayed to be able to provide the bedroom suite for her Christmas. Not only, did Stephanie receive the exact same suit she prayed for; but she also received all the accessories, which went with it! God always provides more than we ask from Him, exceedingly, abundantly more!

God pays extremely close attention to every little detail of our lives, not only for our needs, but also for all our hopes, our dreams and our desires. He desires to give us exceedingly, abundantly, above all that we could ask or think according to the power that works in us. I used to think that meant our power, but it does not. It means God's power working in and through us.

That day, God had already surpassed anything I could have imagined He would do with the seed I planted. First, there was our dinner, then a hundred dollar bill pressed into my hand, and now Stephanie had been given her very own bedroom suite, along with all the frills. To my amazement, God was not through, yet!

Later that afternoon, two couples from our church family came to our apartment. They brought Stephanie a CD player, a television, and an entertainment center. They placed a CD player, which they wrapped beautifully, underneath the tree for her to have Christmas morning.

If that was not enough, do you remember my friend's car that broke down? The Spirit of God was moving on them to pay for having the friend's car fixed and to replace the stolen stereo. God also provided a nice little car through one of the couples, which was the car I mentioned earlier in the book. They told me I could have it as long as I needed it. Before they left, they placed a check in my hand. Both couples were so gracious in their giving in every area. The light at the end of this long, dark tunnel seemed to become brighter and brighter.

There was absolutely no way to measure the blessings of the Lord that day! The blessings in money alone were approximately five hundred dollars. I was blessed that I was able to pay some bills and buy gifts for Christmas. Furthermore, they blessed me with a vehicle, repaired my friend's car and replaced the stereo. Stephanie's bedroom was completely furnished, along with the television, the CD player, and the entertainment center. The countless blessings also included the joys of seeing my children open their presents. However, overall, the most important thing was to experience the loving faithfulness of God. "But my God shall supply all your need, according to His riches in glory by Christ Jesus" (Philippines 4:19, KJV). Jesus Christ said that He came that we might have abundant

86

life, which means in abundance, to the fullest measure, until it overflows into every area of our lives. "I am come that they might have life, and that they might have it more abundantly" (John 10:10, KJV).

If not for God, it probably would have been the most depressing Christmas ever, filled with disappointment, disbelief, and a feeling of unworthiness. Instead, it was a Christmas of miracles! This was a Christmas of excitement and delight. It was a time of signs, miracles, and wonders! It was another Christmas where God showed up and showed out! God always comes through, He is never too late; He is always on time. He can be trusted with our most intimate needs and desires. Even when no one else knows what you are praying for, God hears and knows all. Not only does He hear; but He also answers!

Neither one of us would have appreciated the provision, nor would it have had the impact on our lives that it did, if I could have provided within myself. Our faith dramatically increased through this display of God's never-ending love.

QUESTIONS FOR REFLECTION

Have you fully trusted God with your needs and desires?

What have you trusted God to do for you?

What has God done for you in which you are thankful?

Here is a good exercise for you to try: Write in a journal the blessings for which you are most grateful. Years ago, I began writing in my journal to thank God for all His many blessings. My journal transformed into a Prayer Journal. Every now and then, I read them again. It is so amazing to see, how many prayers God has answered, and the awesome way in which He answered!

PRAYER

Father, .

I am truly grateful for all You have done, for all you are now doing, and for all You are going to accomplish in my life and the lives of my loved ones. I pray I will never forget to thank You and praise You for Your many blessings. Encourage me to keep a journal so that I may refer back to it from time to time, and recount the numerous prayers, which have been answered. These things I ask in the name of Jesus. Amen.

Marriage and Divorce

*F*irst of all, let me clarify to you that I am not an advocate for divorce. I learned early in life, it is biblically, until death do you part. Yet, I found myself in a divorce after three children and twenty-three years of marriage.

This separation did not come quickly. We lived separate lives for many years, though we remained married. Separation and divorce usually comes very subtly.

Disobedience to the word of God was our first and worst mistake we could have made. The Bible, "basic instructions before leaving earth," is our manual for a joyful and successful life. The Word teaches us not to be unequally yoked together, especially with an unbeliever. Just thought you might like to know the definition of unequal. It means not measurably the same, and not of the same social position, meaning status, rank, or position, not evenly matched. The definition for yoked means harnessed together; people or animals bound or tied to each other; to be joined or linked together; steering; and bearing the burden. Do you get the picture I am trying to paint here?

> Be ye not unequally yoked together with unbelievers, for what fellowship hath righteousness with unrighteousness? And what communion hath light with darkness?
>
> 2 Corinthians 6:14 (KJV)

If you are planning marriage in your future, make sure you hear from the Holy Spirit. If you should hear a still, small voice that tells you to wait or run, please listen to the Spirit of God. If you are a child of God, you will know His voice. Listen and obey!

For you see, this is where my disobedience started. I heard the voice of the Holy Spirit so clearly. Only, I did not obey Him. I heard the Lord say, "Do not marry him until he surrenders his life to Me."

My second mistake was thinking we loved each other so much, that my love for him would cause him to want to serve the Lord, to surrender his life to Him. My third mistake was thinking I could change him. Of course, none of the above was true. Please, take advice from someone who knows, you cannot change anyone but yourself. Even with that assignment, we have to have God's help. Thinking you can change someone else will turn out to be merely a fantasy. You will only be deceiving yourself.

Now, I am not saying that our marriage was all bad, because it was not. Our marriage produced three beautiful children. We just grew apart, and were in two very different worlds. We were unequally yoked! Although he believed in God, we still had very different belief systems. He wanted the worldly things, and I wanted the spiritual.

As I said earlier, I am far from being a saint, by any stretch of the imagination. After we married, I stopped going to church for a few years. I was trying to serve God and be in the world at the same time. That will never work! I soon found out I could not have it both ways. You cannot serve two masters; you will love one and hate the other.

No man can serve two masters; for either he will hate the one and love the other, or else he will hold to the one and despise the other.

Matthew 6:24 (KJV)

I realize this is in reference to mammon, but I feel it may also apply to other situations. God says to get off the fence and choose whom you will serve. He says if you are lukewarm, you make Him sick. "So then because thou art lukewarm, and neither cold nor hot, I will spew (vomit) thee out of My mouth" (Revelation 3:16, KJV). Yes, He would rather you be hot, or even cold, than to be just lukewarm!

Through trials, tribulations, and the difficulties of everyday life, raising three children, through miscarriages and abortion, through almost losing our children in a car accident and, in later years, our son, ripped from us and put in prison, our marriage was spiraling downhill. The marriage did not fail due to one thing or another. It was the weight of everything, along with no communication, no quality time together, no spiritual compatibility or mutual goals for our life together. We just co-existed day by day.

I had gotten to the point where I thought if I did not get out of that marriage, I would lose my mind, my salvation, or both. Looking back, I believe I blamed my husband for our son being in prison. In retrospect, I think I just needed someone to blame. He just happened to be in the line of fire. For this, I have asked the Father for forgiveness. I also ask for his forgiveness and the forgiveness of our children. I realize now, it was not his fault alone. We both did things that hurt each other. The main thing we need to remember is this fact: we wrestle against principalities and powers, not flesh and blood. Satan is your enemy, not your spouse!

Now ladies, it is good to have your own interests and to have fellowship with godly women, but be careful that you do not start leading separate lives from your husband. One of our biggest problems was that we had different priorities. Our interests were definitely different, with dissimilar goals and dreams.

My goal and dream was to serve the Lord together and raise our children to love and serve the Lord, also. I tried to teach them the word of God, to bring them up in the house of God, and most importantly, to bring them up to be the Church. By this, I mean, to have an intimate relationship with Jesus Christ. His philosophy was that you did not have to attend church to be saved. In the Word it states, "Forsake not the assembling of yourselves together."

In my opinion, the thing, which finally destroyed our marriage, was the fact that we would not or could not forgive one another. When I did not forgive, it became a part of my life that opened the door for the enemy to come in to steal, kill, and destroy what was left of our marriage. "The thief cometh not but to steal and to kill and to destroy" (John 10:10, KJV). First, went the joy, then peace, and finally, our marriage.

Looking back, there was a lot we both could have done to make our marriage better. I am sure we both have regrets. Our marriage did not have to end in divorce; but I had hardened my heart. At the time, I felt like I could not forgive. Later, I realized the forgiveness was more for me than for him. Many times, I have prayed that he and our children could find it in their hearts to forgive me for splitting up our home.

After our divorce, I was deceived into believing, I was being shunned or alienated from the church I was attending. I know now that also was an attack of the enemy. The enemy was playing with my mind, telling me, I was not a whole person. My self-worth was extremely low. How could I expect my children and God to forgive me for being divorced and for tearing our family apart?

I am talking about a person who had been in church as long as I can remember. I had been taught about the love, grace, and mercy of God's forgiveness. I knew the story of the "woman at the well." Yet, with all of this head knowledge, my heart had amnesia! It is hard to explain, but it was as if Satan had managed to hide this truth from me.

One day I burst into tears with joy and gladness, because I heard the Lord say, "If I forgave the woman at the well for five husbands and the man she was living with, why would I not forgive you for one?" Just one word or one statement can and will change your life forever more, if you will only hearken to His voice. *If not for God,* I would still feel as if I was not forgiven and unworthy. I would still be walking around, deceived by the enemy. I am pleased to say, God has healed me through the power of forgiveness; therefore, I am able to earnestly, pray for him and his spouse. We all have a good relationship, which is extremely necessary when you have children and grandchildren.

In closing, if you are contemplating divorce, I urge you to seek God's face, in order that His perfect will be accomplished, not yours. As I am writing this, I am extremely aware of relationships where it could be a life or death situation. In those times, I admonish you to be intently aware of the Holy Spirit and His leading. In the other cases, I would say do everything within your power to restore your marriage, starting with allowing God to do all that is in His power. Let me say, there are many consequences you, your children, and your grandchildren will face due to divorce, things you cannot foresee now. Know what the Spirit of God is speaking about your particular situation.

QUESTIONS FOR REFLECTION

Are you living a life where you want the best of both worlds?

Would God spew you out of His mouth? Are you warm, cold, or lukewarm in your relationship with Him?

Do you and your spouse have the same beliefs, goals and dreams?

Have you sincerely prayed for your marriage and your spouse?

Are you allowing God to change your spouse instead of trying to change him yourself?

Have you contemplated divorce?

Do you desire the restoration of your marriage?

PRAYER

Father,

I want to be on fire for You. I do not want the things of this world to drag me down with it. I desire to be fully committed, faithful and true in my relationship with You. No more straddling the fence between the world and Your kingdom. I ask, Lord, that You bless my husband, teach him, mold him into whom, You want him to be, not what I think he should be. Change the things in my life, which need to be changed as well. Give me wisdom, knowledge and understanding where my marriage is concerned. Teach me to pray for him instead of condemning him. I pray that our goals, dreams and visions become one with You. Strengthen our love for one another, and help us to be quick to forgive. Remind us, so we will not allow the sun to go down before we settle our differences. Destroy all barriers; destroy all foolish pride before it destroys our marriage and our family. Restore our marriage greater than it has ever been before. I ask this in Your name Jesus. Amen.

Marriage and Death

*T*his period was extremely difficult and heart wrenching to say the least. It was a very hard time in my life and the lives of many others involved. Please understand; my intention is not to bring hurt, shame, or sorrow to anyone. My only intention is to bring healing to others who may have been through the same type of situation, or those who may face a similar situation now or in the future.

The family I married into, I loved very much and still do to this day. My father-in-law was more like a father to me, and the only grandfather my youngest daughter has ever really known. He is full of spiritual wisdom and was a great source of strength for us in our time of need. There is really no way to express the love and support this family gave us.

There are many things I still have to deal with today. I am sure there are others dealing with issues, too. I will not pretend to understand all that took place over this five-year period; but I will say, "God is faithful!"

Approximately two-and-a-half years after my divorce, I met my second husband through friends in my church. We had the same belief system. I was very confident, this time that we were equally yoked.

He was a man that loved the Lord with all his heart. We believed God put us together. Several people had spoken prophecy over us before we were married, that God had ordained our marriage. Prophecy had been spoken over us more times than I could count that we had a ministry together. They say love is blind; but my opinion is that love is deaf, dumb, and blind! Believe it! There is more truth packed in that little statement than you could ever imagine! When you love someone, you do not see what others may see.

During the course of our marriage, we endured many attacks of the enemy. Little did I know when I married him, the demonic battles he was facing and the attacks that lay ahead. Trust me, whatever demonic forces your spouse contends with, you will, too. The ways of attack might be different; but the battle is still evident. It is crucial for you to know and understand your enemy. That only comes from the Word, from the teaching of the Holy Spirit and, unfortunately, from experience.

There are those who would question me as to how in heaven could this marriage have been from God. Even now, my husband, Tom, tells me there is no way this could have been from God. I, to this day, do not understand it, either. I only know it was for a time and a season. One thing I can honestly say is that it did bring in much spiritual growth.

To some of you, this may sound crazy. One day, I was crying out to God to help me understand why He would allow me to be so blind, and why He would allow me to enter a marriage of such torment. Especially, since I had prayed for over two years, and waited and sought God with all my heart for the husband He handpicked just for me.

At that moment, I heard a soft, gentle voice reply back to me, "If you had known, you would not have married him, and that was not My plan." I was thinking, *Okay, God, what is Your plan?* However, I did not hear another response. Sometimes we just have to trust God to lead us, even when we cannot hear Him.

All I know to say is whatever you go through, whatever you endure in this lifetime; it will be of use to help someone else go through it. If you have questioned what your ministry is, therein rests your answer. God's desire is to use you in the areas where you have been used and abused, where you have received wounds. Who better to bring healing to someone than someone who has fought that battle and was victorious? There is nothing new under the sun or the Son! How can we help someone if we cannot relate to his or her feelings, fears, failures, circumstances, and situations? Besides, I have always heard it said, "What doesn't kill you makes you stronger!" Like it or not, this statement is so true to life.

As I said before, my daughter, Stephanie, and I did not know what we were facing. My husband had a tremendous amount of health problems, which resulted in addiction to prescription drugs. He managed to hide this extremely well. He looked like a picture of health!

A word to the wise, just because a doctor or physician prescribes a medication, that does not mean you cannot become addicted to it. When the doctors realized he was addicted, instead of helping him overcome the addiction, they just cut him off.

This opened up a world of other problems. Now, he had to seek other sources to obtain the drugs his body was craving. If he took the drugs, he was sick. If he could not get the drugs, he was sick, because his body would start to go through withdrawals. It was so severe that it had gotten to a point where he would have two or three days a week that were good. The other four or five days, he was extremely ill.

During these times, his temper would become very volatile, particularly when it concerned Stephanie and me. Suddenly, without warning, his temperament would change. It was like turning on and off a light switch! He became very abusive mentally, physically, and emotionally.

When he was good, you could not ask for better. He was in his right mind and serving the Lord to the best of his ability. When he was bad, he was demonically controlled; due to that fact, he opened the door through the addiction. It reminds me of what Paul said in Romans, "For the good that I would do, I do not; but the evil which I would not do, that I do" (Romans 7:19, KJV). You see, it was not that he wanted to do these things, but demonic forces drove him. Please understand, I am not saying he was demon possessed, because that is not my intention. The fact of the matter is that some drugs are mind altering, which allows the forces of evil to influence us. In other words, it opens the door for the demonic forces to influence our mind, will, and emotions.

Ephesians 6 speaks about the "whole armor of God," and tells you of the enemy that is against you:

> Put on all of God's armor so that you will be able to stand firm against all strategies and tricks of the devil. For we are not fighting against people made of flesh and blood, but against the evil rulers and authorities of the unseen world, against those mighty powers of darkness who rule this world, and against wicked spirits in the heavenly realm.
>
> Ephesians 6:11-12 (NLT)

Principalities, powers of darkness and evil, constantly attacked him. Their assignment was to destroy his ministry and kill him. His spiritual insight was phenomenal. He could see angelic beings, both heavenly and demonic. It astounded me that he was not able to push back the forces of evil. He had prophetic dreams and visions that manifested in the natural. Through one of his dreams, Pastors Dell and Jill Young accepted the call to ministry and birthed a wonderful church ministry, Cornerstone Christian Church in Sparks, Georgia. I can truly say the pastors and the church have been a great blessing in our lives.

Once, my husband shared with me about an incident that happened to him when he was approximately five years old. He said he was extremely sick with one illness, right after another. He was not sure if it was a dream or a vision he experienced, but in his dream (or vision), he woke up and a tremendous being was carrying him in His arms. The being was a beautiful, bright light with shafts of light extending from Him. The light was so bright; he could not actually see His face. He was dressed in a long, white robe.

He asked the being where He was taking him. He said He was taking Him to heaven to be with God and Jesus. As a little boy, he did not understand and just wanted to be with his daddy and mommy. He told the heavenly Host or (what he then believed to be the Holy Spirit) that he wanted to go home. He explained to him that if He took him back home, he would be very sick and go through many terrible things in his life. He then asked the heavenly Host if he would go to heaven if he stayed home. He told him, yes, he would go to heaven. He then told the heavenly Host, he wanted his mommy and daddy. The next thing he knew, he woke up in his bed.

Indeed, he did suffer many things in his lifetime. He had cancer, breathing problems, acid reflux disease, and many other attacks. He was in a constant state of severe pain. I can remember, for days at a time, we would be at the hospital. One week in particular, we went to the hospital every single night for hours at a time. The rest of the night, I would massage his back and his legs, so he could get some relief from the pain. Even though I was up most of the night, I had to be at work the next morning. For months, I managed to sleep a few minutes here, an hour or two there. Our lives began to accelerate from bad to worse!

Fear began to enter my mind and the mind of my daughter. Praying and seeking the Holy Spirit was our only avenue of protection. There were times when the Holy Spirit would speak to me, or I would just have urgency, in my spirit, to get out of the house.

Other times, there were people who would call and warn me that the Holy Spirit said to grab some clothes and leave. I knew there was a potential for danger. Finally, it got to the point where I kept a little money, an extra key to my car, a couple of changing of clothes for Stephanie and myself, toothbrushes, toothpaste, deodorant, some makeup, and a hairbrush; you know, the necessities of life. We had our own little emergency bag tucked safely in the trunk of the car.

There were times when I did not heed the warnings, or I did not leave in time. Those times were the worst of all. There were nights when he would lock me in our bedroom. Thank God, Stephanie was spending the night with friends at these particular times. Not only would he lock me in the bedroom, but also he would literally take the light bulbs out of the room, so that I would be in total darkness. *If not for God,* I would have lost my sanity. It was extremely difficult being there at night, in the dark, not knowing what would take place next. I slept only by dozing. I learned quickly to hide a flashlight, batteries and the Bible underneath the bed.

Whether just threatened or the threat was carried out, we suffered numerous attacks, spiritually, mentally, emotionally, financially, and physically. There were times when he would literally push us out of the house. My daughter would stay with a friend while I would find a place elsewhere. On many occasions, I would go stay with my oldest daughter, Mandi. In addition, friends blessed me, who would let me stay with them and even allowed us to stay in their camper. Twice, I received the offer of a house to live in if I would pay the electric bill. We were truly blessed with people who cared, and for that, I am thankful!

On numerous occasions, I actually stayed at my place of employment. It was a senior citizen's center, and I was the Coordinator. The seniors were only there from about eight in the morning until one in the afternoon. Conveniently, it was equipped with a kitchen, bathroom, TV, and two sofas. I felt so much peace and security when I was there.

My prayer to God was if there was supposed to be a time of separation between us; He would have to supply Stephanie and me a place to live. The position I had was not provision enough to afford a descent place.

The next day, I received a call from a woman I knew. She said her daughter had her house up for sale, but would like someone to stay in the house until she could sell it. All they wanted me to do was pay the electricity bill, the water bill, and keep the yards mowed. It was fully furnished! I am not just talking furniture; I am telling you it had everything down to silverware, glassware, and dishes. The pantry was also stocked. That is so like God, exceedingly, abundantly more than I could think or imagine! God is so wonderfully awesome! He is our provision; He is our answer to everything!

My daughter and I moved in the next day. There was no doubt in my mind that the house was a Godsend. We did not have to come up with the money to turn on the electricity or the water; God had provided those needs. I am telling you, this was an act of God, a supernatural manifestation of His love. To this day, I am truly grateful for the friends and family who were obedient to the voice of God.

We separated for approximately fifteen months. I just had to believe God was working on our behalf. During this time, we kept the communication lines open, but nothing significant was taking place. My social life consisted of spending time with God, children, and grandchildren, going to work and to church. He was still hanging with the same crowds, doing the same things.

He was living at his dad and mom's house, along with his teenage son. In February 2001, his mother collapsed. She had been sick for an extended period with cancer and breathing problems. My husband was there with her and called the ambulance; later that afternoon, she passed away.

That night, my husband completely lost it. He grabbed a shotgun and ran to his mother's bedroom. His intention was to commit suicide. I fought with him while he was trying to load the gun. He was so distraught and nervous that he kept dropping the shells. Each time he would drop the ammunition on the floor, I would manage to kick it under the bed out of his reach. There were several guns in the house and all sorts of different shells and bullets. Thank God, he did not manage to get the right shells!

The police chief was a friend of the family, and we knew him well. The police chief coaxed him into giving him the gun and seeking professional help. He checked himself into the hospital on our anniversary, which was the day after his mother died. His dad and I picked him up from the hospital on February 14th, at which time he went back and stayed at his dad's house.

Later that same month, there were several severe thunderstorms and tornadoes. The day was so dark and dreary; such an overwhelming heaviness was all around us. It was as if you could actually feel the demonic activity in the atmosphere. I knew something was going on; but I could not put my finger on it.

Late that evening, my father-in-law went home to find the house completely dark. My husband's vehicle was in the driveway, so he went to his son's room to find out what was going on. My father-in-law found him lying on the bed, barely breathing. He ran to call an ambulance, only to find the phones were not working. He ran back out to use the phone in his truck. They rushed him to the hospital in a frantic attempt to save his life.

Two of our close friends from church, where my father-in-law was senior pastor, came by and picked up my daughter and me, and took us to the hospital. The Holy Spirit reminded me of what I prayed when my daddy was dying. I began to bind the death angel's hands so he could not take him, and started pleading the blood of

Jesus over him. In fact, we all began to pray that way. There was a whole lot of praying in the Spirit, also!

When we arrived at the hospital, they were not giving us any reason to hope. To be frank, they told us to be prepared for the worst. However, that did not deter us from believing that God was still God and He was in control! I remember thinking, whose report are you going to believe?

The doctor, who was trying to revive him, had been working on him for over thirty minutes. She said he was not breathing, and there was no pulse. She informed us she had done all she could possibly do. We insisted she keep trying. At that point, another doctor came in to assist her.

They had already pronounced him dead, oh, but God intervened! In fact, he was revived after what seemed like an hour. Still the doctors were not optimistic at all. They finally found a heartbeat, but he was unable to breathe on his own. He was on a respirator, which they said was keeping him alive; but we knew better! It was only by the grace of God that he was breathing. They informed us if he lived, he would probably be unable to function mentally, physically, and emotionally. They advised us that he might not know who we were, and may not be able to walk or talk. At best, he would have to learn to walk and talk all over again. You see, he was in a coma, physically, but not spiritually!

As soon as he was stable enough to transport, they sent him to another hospital in a town approximately twenty-five miles away. They had to use a hand respirator for him to receive the oxygen to survive the trip. We followed the ambulance to the hospital.

Shortly after he arrived, they inserted a breathing tube down his throat and gave him medicine to paralyze his body, so he could not rip the tubing from his throat. He was in intensive care for fifteen days. He battled many, many setbacks, including pneumonia, during that course of time.

Thank God, we had many people praying for our family. The Word was spoken over him, constantly. Also in his room, I kept the television turned to a channel, which only aired scripture, and praise and worship music. We believed he was healed. In my heart I knew, while he was in the coma, he was talking and walking with Jesus.

Practically the only time, I left the hospital was when I went home to get fresh clothing and to check on Stephanie. She was staying with a friend. Toward the end of his stay at the hospital, even though he was still in a coma, his vital signs seemed to be getting better. He was still on the respirator, but he started breathing more on his own. I started back to work, but would go straight to the hospital around one o'clock each day.

One day, when I arrived at the hospital, they told me he was out of the coma, and they had taken out the breathing tube. However, at the same time, they warned me not to expect too much. They cautioned me he might not know me, he may not be able to walk or talk. Now, came the moment of truth!

Trembling all over, I walked into the room, praying, "God, it is up to you." When I walked in, his head turned toward me. I stopped, dead in my tracks. I asked him, "Do you know who I am?"

He smiled very big and said, "Of course, I know who you are," and then he reached out to hug and kiss me. Then he said, "It's been a long time since I've kissed you!" My questions about amnesia and his ability to talk were answered at that very moment. Although, he was extremely weak, he was able to walk almost immediately.

After we hugged and kissed, all he could talk about was Jesus. He could not say enough about the love that exuded from Him. He just kept exclaiming, "Do you know, how much love He is? There is so much love in Him! There is so much love, coming out of Him! He is pure, radiant light! There are not enough words to express, how great His love is! Jesus and I walked and talked with each other. He told me I had to go back and tell everyone I could about the immeasurable love that was within Him. I told Him, I did not want to go back; I wanted to stay there with Him. But He said I had to come back and tell them about His love and that He was coming soon."

He also spoke about the beautiful colors; he spoke of their brilliance. He told everyone that came in his room about Jesus. He witnessed to them about the love of Jesus Christ, and the fact that He is coming soon! Jesus is love, the greatest and purest love of all!

A few days later, they released him from the hospital; but our journey did not end there. Due to the amount of pills they found in his stomach and lungs, they assumed he tried to commit suicide again. Therefore, by law, they required him to enter a mental hospital for observation. He told the police chief and the doctors that he did not try to commit suicide; but to no avail.

At the time this incident took place, he was working with the police chief as an informant, in order to help eliminate some of the drug trafficking in that area. On that particular day, he stated three people came to the house, two men and a woman. He knew all three of them because he had dealt with them before this time. He also stated the two men held him down, while the woman injected him with a drug. Then they proceeded to shove pills down his throat. One of the intruders said, "It won't be long, now." In other words, it was attempted murder, not suicide! His story seemed to make sense, especially when one of the neighbors noticed an unfamiliar vehicle in the driveway and the phones were working that morning, but not that evening. There are those who think he did try to commit suicide; but to this day, I do not and neither does his family.

Not a soul was brought in for the attempted murder. Law enforcement told us the assailants only received a slap on the hand and were advised to leave the area, which led me to believe the law was involved in the whole conspiracy. I believe that God is a God of justice, and justice will come to all parties involved!

When my husband came home from the hospital, we found a house and reconciled our marriage. We were happy for a while, but the drug dealers would not leave him alone. They knew he was an easy target due to pain, sickness, and disease. Talking about being bold, they would even go to his place of employment. They were relentless in their pursuit to sell him drugs.

Once again, he was determined to take them off the streets. He called one of the police officers that attended our church. Upon explaining to the officer about what was going on, they decided to call in the narcotics division. Two officers came to our home and spoke with my husband to set up a sting operation. They asked me to leave the room, because they did not want me involved in any way. I begged him not to get involved, because I knew his life would be in danger, and it could be a threat to my daughter and me. He felt this was his only chance to get free; therefore, he proceeded with the investigation. The only thing I could do was pray for protection.

My memories are vague at this point; but I do remember the officers would call him for meetings. One day he received another call from the officers, requesting a meeting. During the time he was gone, I received a phone call from one of the known drug dealers. He threatened my husband and stated he had better not show up at his house ever again. This threat terrified me! I did not know what this person might do. I prayed until my husband came home. Come to find out, the officers from narcotics had him wired and sent him to the drug dealer's house. He said he knew they had caught on to what he was doing. He was fearful for his life, but he was still determined to stop them

Right after this took place that same feeling of demonic activity was in the atmosphere again. The very same heaviness I felt before, when the attempted murder took place, seemed to overshadow us. The night seemed so strange and eerie. There was a terrible storm that night. The electricity was off all over the whole town. Keep in mind; this was on a Monday night.

I retired early that night, but my husband stayed up. I had a horrible dream. It was one of those dreams where you are not sure if you are awake or dreaming. It was so real, so tangible!

The dream: There was this horrifying creature standing in front of me. This demonic creature had a mask covering his face. In my dream, I knew this thing could not hurt me; but he was torturing me by the evilness of his appearance. Suddenly, boldness surrounded me; the fear was gone as I reached over and snatched the mask off its face. In the process of removing the mask, I was saying, "You cannot deceive me, I know who you are!" However, underneath the mask was a face more terrifying, more demonic than before. I woke up screaming, crying, trembling, and I was drenched with perspiration.

My husband came running into the room to find out what was wrong. When I was able to get my composure, I told him about the dream. His words were, "I do not understand what it means, but I know it was a warning from God." I prayed and asked God what it meant, but did not get an answer at that time.

On Friday morning, four days after the dream, I started to leave for work when I felt a tugging in my spirit to go back and tell my husband I loved him one more time. I am so thankful I listened to the Spirit. He told me he loved Stephanie and me, and we both apologized for some things, we had said the night before. Afterward, I went on to work.

As I said earlier, I was the Coordinator/Director of the senior center in our county. Part of our responsibility was delivering meals to the elderly. One of our drivers brought the meals back to the center stating she could not deliver the meals because law enforcement had that particular area locked down. They would not allow anyone to enter or leave that area.

At that very moment, I had that feeling of dreadful fear come over me, again. I tried to call my husband. Somehow, I knew they were having a drug bust, even though my husband had not breathed one word of it. I could not reach him, but that was not unusual. When he would go into a state of depression, he would shut himself off from everything and everybody. He had been in that state of mind for the last few days.

I received a call at work later on in the day, but all they would do was breathe in the phone. I thought it might be my husband; I called his name, but there was not a response. The phone clicked, and then only the dial tone could be heard.

I nearly went home at lunchtime, but I needed to finish all the reports the county and government required for the end of the month. I called home around four o'clock that afternoon. Still no answer, so I left a message on the answering machine. I told my husband I was going to run by the county office to take the reports and then go to the grocery store. I let him know I would be home around five o'clock, and I also told him I loved him.

I arrived home between five or five thirty that evening. I blew the horn to let him know I was home, because he would normally help me with the groceries. He did not come out, so I came on in the house, calling his name; but he did not answer. We had glass sliding doors leading out to the patio. I saw him lying on his side with his back up against the glass doors. I then noticed our cat standing beside him. My first thought was he was playing with the cat, because he loved that crazy cat. I even made a remark to him about playing with the cat. Then I realized his head was on the pile of firewood. My next thought was that he had fallen and hit his head on the wood. I, immediately, dropped the groceries on the floor and ran to him, calling out his name. Still there was no answer. I remember kneeling down beside him, talking to him. In my heart, I knew he was gone. However, in an attempt to save him, to bring him back again as before, I ran to call an ambulance. However, I could not find the phone. Desperately, I ran outside to find help.

There was a business across the street from our home. It was after-hours, but there were men mowing the lawn. I tried frantically to get their attention by screaming out to them, but they could not hear. Then a woman passed by in her car. Apparently, she saw that I was very upset. She stopped and asked what was wrong. I explained to her that I needed an ambulance for my husband, because he had fallen. The next thing I knew, my neighbors were by my side. My neighbor could barely understand me as I was telling her what had happened, because I was so hysterical.

Someone called an ambulance. In the meantime, my neighbors and I went back to see about my husband. As I started out the patio door, the woman pulled me back into the house. I did not understand what she was doing; therefore, I kept trying to go to him. She would not allow me to go back out there. I kept saying I have to go to him; I have to help him! Then is when she told me he was dead, and I could not help him. She proceeded to tell me, someone had shot him. I could not believe what I was hearing!

Later, I found out she was protecting me. She asked me if I had touched the gun or my husband. My response was, "What gun?" I know that God was protecting me, also. You see, the gun was lying right beside him. Even though I knelt down next to him, I did not remember seeing the gun. I do not know if I actually did not see the gun, or if my mind was protecting me by blocking it out. By the way, the reason, I could not find the phone was because it was lying on the patio.

He died the afternoon of the morning of the drug bust. Coincidence, I think not! The officer he was working with on the drug investigation was at our home that day. When he came to check on me, I literally begged him to find my husband's murderers. I knew it must be in relation to the drug bust. The law enforcement team would not let them move the body until the officer from the

Georgia Bureau of Investigation arrived at the crime scene. It was nearly 2 a.m. before he arrived. I stayed there the entire time; I just could not bring myself to leave him there, all alone.

The investigator asked me all sorts of questions. He wanted to know all the specifics and where I was when all this took place. He wanted to know if I had an alibi. He asked me if I had touched the gun or the body. That I could not say for sure. I did not think I did, but I did not even remember seeing a gun. I did not know at the time, but the spouse is always under suspicion.

The GBI agent ruled my husband's death as suicide. I know in my heart and spirit that it was a lie from the pits of hell! There were just too many things, which pointed more toward murder than suicide. The agent chose not to believe, or someone coerced him into believing, that his decision was correct. I am still not convinced; I feel like there was protection implemented for higher-ups; if you know what I mean?

First, my husband wore a wire when he went into the drug den with people who knew him very well, knew where he lived, and where he worked. There were threats made to me, personally, threats left on our answering machine, and the other weird calls made to our home, talking about someone bleeding to death. I begged them to investigate the calls; but they never did. There was a drug bust that morning. Approximately two hours later, he was shot!

Sometime in between the drug bust and his death, he drove across town, broke into his dad's gun cabinet, and took a shotgun. He then drove back to our home. I believe, with all my heart, he took the gun for protection, not for suicide. The patio door was open just enough to squeeze through it. The portable phone was on the patio, and not working when we found it. We tried to charge it so we could see who called him last or see whom he called. My father-in-law checked it, because it would never charge up. We then found that someone had unplugged the phone battery on the inside of the phone. There was no reason for my husband to have unplugged the battery, because if he did not want to answer it, he just would not have answered. Keep in mind, the last time he nearly died, someone had tampered with the phones.

He had been shot in the chest with a shotgun. Most people that commit suicide with that type of weapon usually use their feet, according to my research. He was wearing his shoes, and his feet, ankles and knees were in perfect alignment. It was as though his body had been arranged in that position. No, I do not believe for one moment that this was a suicide!

A couple of weeks after his death, naturally, I had been crying out to God to show me whether it was suicide or murder. There were people who said I just did not want to accept the reality of his suicide. Therefore, I sought God, because I needed some type of closure. The Holy Spirit brought back to my remembrance the dream I had on that Monday night before his death on Friday. Do you remember the demonic creature with the mask? I believe God was telling me do not be deceived, he did not kill himself; he was murdered!

About the same time of this revelation, I had another dream. I was sitting in a rocking chair. My husband was sitting on the floor, resting his head on my lap. In my dream, I knew he was gone, but he was comforting me. I asked him if he had done this to himself. His response to me was, "No, Sweetie, I did not do this." His voice was so reassuring and peaceful. Immediately I woke up, but with the peace, that passes all understanding. It has been settled in my spirit ever since.

I know in my spirit he is in heaven, walking and talking with Jesus today. You see, it does not matter, the struggles you go through here on this earth. The most important thing is your confession of faith in Jesus Christ, as your Lord and Savior. God knows the intent of the heart. My husband's desire was to be totally set free and serve the Lord with all of his heart.

Even though we may fail miserably at times, we need to pick ourselves back up and place one foot in front of the other. The Word says the righteous will fall, not may fall, but will fall! The awesome part is that the righteous gets back up. Do not focus on the numerous times you may have fallen, because God looks on the times you managed to rise again! If we can make it one step at a time, and keep our trust in Jesus, we will make it! This, ladies, is the unconditional and unfathomable love of Jesus Christ and the power of His blood!

In retrospect, many things had happened, both good and evil. However, know this, good always prevails over evil. With God, there is not a good deed or an evil deed that goes unnoticed.

> The eyes of the Lord are in every place, beholding the evil and the good.
>
> Proverbs 15:3 (KJV)

> Whoso rewardeth (returns) evil for good, evil shall not depart from his house.
>
> Proverbs 17:13 (KJV)

> For God shall bring every work into judgment, including every secret thing, whether it be good or whether it be evil.
>
> Ecclesiastes 12:14 (KJV)

You will receive forgiveness if you are sincere in your asking. However, I remind you: you will reap what you sow. Rest assured; you will receive your just desserts!

Thank God, He was watching over me and protecting me. God was using other people, also, sending them to protect me. Please know, He is always working, even though we may not see it. We may never know the situations or circumstances where God intervened. Sometimes, we are blessed enough that He reveals them to us a little further down the path of life.

Remember, I almost went home at lunchtime that day. I guess I will not know until I reach heaven if God was protecting me from being murdered along with my husband, or if He was protecting me from being falsely accused for his murder. Not only did he protect me then; but also there were witnesses if I needed them. The woman who worked in the same building with me could verify where I was at the time. In addition, I saw and spoke with the officer my husband was working with and his wife at the grocery store. *If not for God,* where would I be today? Either way, I am so thankful I have a Savior who cares for me! One who knows every detail of my life.

Ordinarily, Stephanie would have returned home from school before I arrived home. Thank God, it was on a Friday afternoon and she had planned to spend the night with a friend. Again, I thank my God that He spared her the agony of finding her stepfather the way I found him.

There are many things I have repented of during this marriage. I was far from being the "perfect wife." There were times, when I chose church over my spouse. Understand I am not talking about choosing God, I mean church! Nevertheless, there were times; I was in church when he needed me. My priorities were not in order. God created the institution of marriage and family long before He instituted the church.

At times, I walked in the flesh instead of with the Spirit. As you are walking through trials, Satan and flesh will show you all the ways you are persecuted. I have repeatedly gone over this time in my life, analyzing and dissecting every part of it, in an effort to find out what I should or should not have done, so that there might have been a different outcome. So many times, I questioned God and self if I had done all that was in my power to help him. When we allow ourselves to walk in the flesh, it only serves to hinder, hurt, and destroy. If we walk in the Spirit, then it serves to heal and restore. When you walk in the flesh, you will walk in your own purpose, fulfilling the desires of the flesh. However, if you choose to walk in the Spirit, you will reveal and fulfill the heart of God!

It took me a long time to be able to forgive myself, not to mention the people that I know were involved. I prayed to my Father in heaven, asking Him to give me the strength to forgive. Little by little, I was able to pray for them, that they might repent and ask for forgiveness for themselves.

My desire is to leave you with a positive perspective. I have a devotional book, *God Calling*, which I read daily. On the day my husband died, for some reason I did not read it. Approximately a week later, the Holy Spirit prompted me to go back and read the passage for that day. I believe, without a shadow of doubt, this was a special message from the Father to me. After you read it, I am convinced you will agree. It read:

February 1
Another Start
Take courage. Do not fear. Start a new life tomorrow.
Put the old mistakes away, and start anew. I give you a fresh
start. Be not burdened. Be not anxious. If My forgiveness
were for the righteous only, and those who had not sinned,
where would be its need?
Remember as I said, "To whom much is forgiven,
the same loveth much."
Why do you fret and worry so? I wait to give you all that is
lovely, but your lives are soiled with worry and fret.
You would crush My treasures.
I can only bless glad, thankful hearts. You must be glad and joyful.
God Calling, February 1

You see, every one of us goes through things in life, which we would not choose to endure. However, here is a Word from the Lord, which may make it a little less painful. God's Word promises: It will be worth it all in the end!

So humble yourselves under the mighty power of God, and in His good time He will honor you. Give all your worries and cares to God, for He cares about what happens to you. Be

114

careful! Watch out for attacks from the devil, your great enemy. He prowls around like a roaring lion, looking for some victim to devour. Take a firm stand against him, and be strong in your faith. Remember that your Christian brothers and sisters all over the world are going through the same kind of suffering you are. In His kindness, God called you to His eternal glory by means of Jesus Christ. After you have suffered a little while, He will restore, support, and strengthen you, and He will place you on a firm foundation. All power is His forever and ever. Amen.

1 Peter 5:6-11 (NLT)

QUESTIONS FOR REFLECTION

Do you continue to trust God, even though, you do not understand or when He seems to be silent?

Reflect back over the course of your life; have there been times when you realized you were under God's protection; although you were not aware, you needed protecting?

Can you recall occasions when the Holy Spirit protected you by giving you a warning?

Do you have your priorities in order?

When you are facing the fiery trials of life, do you feel, as if, you are the only one who has endured that much suffering, pain or heartache?

Have you sincerely prayed for your enemies?

Are you strong and trusting enough to place all your fears, needs, and desires, your hopes and dreams into the hands of God?

PRAYER

Father,

Although, I do not understand why, I am going through these fiery trials; I relinquish full control to You. I trust You to see me through them. Even when I am unable to hear Your voice, keep me strong, so I will not waiver in my faith. Help me to understand I am never alone for You are always with me. Bring to my remembrance all the times in my life or the lives of my loved ones, where You protected us, without us knowing, we needed protection. I pray that I will always recognize a word of warning from the Holy Spirit. Instruct me how to set my priorities in the order that is pleasing to You. Lord, this is a difficult hurdle to jump; but give me Your love and compassion, Your mercy and grace so that I will be able to forgive and sincerely pray for my enemies. Give me the strength and the courage to place everything, which concerns me into Your hands. I give You all my fears, and in doing so I ask You to replace them with power, love, and a sound mind. I know the Word states You will meet all my needs and give me the desires of my heart. Fulfill the dreams and visions You have placed on the inside me. Lord, I am trusting in You to fulfill every promise You have made, for You are not a man that You should lie. Amen.

Which Is Worse:
Divorce Or Death?

$\mathcal{M}$any more times than I could count, I have been questioned as to which is worse, a marriage that ends in divorce or the death of a spouse. The people going through a divorce say it would have to be worse. On the other hand, the ones who have lost a spouse to death will say that is more devastating.

Well, I have been through both divorce and death. In all honesty, it is extremely hard to determine the answer to that question. Trust me; they are both very difficult situations to endure. They both take time to heal. There is the old adage, time heals all wounds. I am not so sure, I agree with that philosophy, but what I do know is that Jesus heals all wounds! I do believe that time will ease the hurt and the pain, if we allow the Holy Spirit to have full reign in our lives. We have to turn all sorrow over to Him. We must trust Him to see us through the difficult times in our lives.

Without the Holy Spirit, one is unable to properly deal with divorce or death. You will encounter so many emotions. There are so many things to cope with and try to understand. I am very confident that there are things you will never be able to comprehend. In both circumstances, you will experience some type of grief, even if you are the one who filed for the divorce. You will experience anger toward your spouse, even though your spouse may have passed away. You will also experience remorse, which is a feeling of guilt, regret, compassion, or pity. Hurt and self-pity will also be a part of your emotional process. You will blame yourself, your spouse, or anyone that is available, even God, whether it is a divorce or a death.

Most women face whether or not they can provide for themselves and their children. Feelings of emptiness, loneliness, rejection, and self-worth are huge issues, especially if you are not the bride of Christ. I will address this in more detail in another chapter.

I have actually had people tell me that divorce was worse, especially if you see them with someone else. However, I ask you, is that worse than never being able to talk to them or look upon their face ever again? At least with divorce, you will have the opportunity to resolve issues, ask forgiveness, and receive forgiveness, face to face. Even though in death you can find forgiveness, you will discover there are so many things left unsaid and undone.

You most definitely will have some type of fear or anxiety. My worst fear with the divorce of my first husband and in the death of my second husband was the fear of not knowing, not knowing what to do or what to expect next. However, there again, that has always been my greatest fear. You are at a standstill; it is, as though, you are suspended in time, and you are just waiting. Furthermore, waiting for what? How long will you have to wait? You see, if you know what is going to take place next, then you can make a plan to get on with your life. Whether it is good or whether it seems to be bad, you can go forward. At this point, decisions can be made.

Mind you, this is just my synopsis of the situation. Whether you find yourself, as a divorcee or a widow, the result is the same. Both end in death, because divorce also typifies death. It is a death of a marriage relationship, a union, a commitment, a death of goals and dreams. It is also death to trust, if you are not careful. How do you come to terms with trusting someone who says, "I will love you, always" or "We will be together till death do us part"? The way you do that is you put your trust in God, not man. *If not for God*, I do not know if I could trust anyone enough to love again. This, ladies, I cannot express enough; put your trust and your faith in God, not in man!

If you have been through a divorce or the death of your spouse, not only is the result and the basic emotions you will go through the same, but the answer to see you through it, to comfort you, to provide your needs or desires will always be Jesus Christ! He will never leave you nor forsake you, not only in this lifetime, but also for eternity. "For He hath said, 'I will never leave thee, nor forsake thee'" (Hebrews 13:5, KJV). The good news is that He actually means it!

QUESTIONS FOR REFLECTION

Have you personally endured divorce or death of a spouse?

Have you played the blame-game by rehearsing in your mind all the things you should have done, should not have done or what if this or that? Believe me, you are not the only one who has done this!

If so, what range of emotions did you experience or still experiencing?

Do you feel you are at a standstill in your life, and you do not know where to go or what to do?

Have you sought God for His plan; His direction and guidance?

Have you relinquished all your pain and sorrow, along with your future, to the Healer, Who is Jesus Christ?

PRAYER

Father,

If the person who is reading this has experienced the pain and sorrow of a divorce or the death of their spouse, I ask You to comfort and heal them now in the name of Jesus. I know from my own experience how difficult and overwhelming it can be, when you lose someone. You feel the weight of the world upon your shoulders, especially if you have children. Lord, comfort and heal the children, also. There is such a range of emotions, which they will encounter, move them through these emotions as quickly as possible. I understand that grief is a process to healing; but do not allow them to grieve longer than they should. Enable them to put their trust in You so they may be able to trust others again. Set them free from all harassing and negative questions in their minds. Give them peace that passes all understanding and joy unspeakable and full of glory. Stagnation is no longer allowed; they cannot be controlled by fear. They will have life and life more abundant in every area of their lives. I pray they will seek Your face for Your direction, guidance, and Your perfect plan for their lives in Jesus Name. Amen.

Oil of Joy

To appoint unto them that mourn in Zion, to give unto them
beauty for ashes, the oil of joy for mourning, the garment of
praise for the spirit of heaviness; that they might be called
trees of righteousness, the planting of the Lord, that He may
be glorified.

Isaiah 61:3 (KJV)

After my husband's death, there was so much with which to deal.
We had very many overwhelming decisions to make, quickly. I had
to find another home. Obviously, my daughter and I did not want
to stay there and even if we had wanted to, we could not afford it.
I had a part-time position and now that we no longer had his sal-
ary to rely on, many changes had to take place. We had two weeks
to find a place and move. After looking at a number of properties,
we found a decent house in a nice neighborhood. God is faithful,
especially since our budget was extremely limited! We had nothing
in the form of finances to fall back on. There were no insurance or
social security benefits.

During the course of those two weeks, I was in the process of
changing occupations to a full-time position, which was a Godsend.
After the loss of my husband, in my quest of searching for a new
residence, moving and starting a new job, along with the financial
strain, it was nearly more than I could handle. In addition, that was

just part of the anxiety; because I had to leave behind the position and people, I dearly loved. However, again, God was truly faithful; therefore, He gave me more people to love through my new position...

Exactly two months to the day of my husband's passing, I woke up, but was unable to get up. I could barely move and was in excruciating pain from my back all the way to my toes. I pinched the sciatic nerve in my back when we moved. I tried for a month to mask the pain by taking ibuprofen, but I was still in terrible pain.

How embarrassing! It took two of my friends and my daughter to cart me to the hospital. The report was since I had let it go on for such a long time, I could become paralyzed. Immediately, we started rebuking the bad report. We decided to believe the report of the Lord, which provides healing in the name of Jesus!

I was in the hospital for approximately two weeks. I could barely get out of bed, and continued to be in a great deal of pain. Oh, but what great friends I had to comfort me during my stay. My family and friends have truly been a blessing to me. I have heard it said, "True friends are like the rainbow, always there for you, even after a storm." If you are fortunate enough to have true friends, you are blessed beyond measure.

Ladies, you know what it is like when you are unable to shower. You just feel dirty, grungy, and much less of a woman. These are what you call the best of friends: They came in all smiles one day, and said they were there to give me a makeover. Make me over, they did! They shampooed my hair, applied my makeup, shaved my legs, and painted my fingernails and toenails. I felt like a new woman! In fact, I felt like I had been resurrected!

During the course of my stay at the hospital, they checked me for other complications I was experiencing. They tried to put colon cancer on me, but we rebuked it in the name of Jesus. Then they said I would have to have back and neck surgery. We rebuked that, too!

One week after leaving the hospital, I went to the hospital for physical therapy on my back and neck. While I was waiting for the therapist to prepare everything, I began feeling pain in my chest. I thought it was just anxiety, or maybe even gas. I started to perspire, and then I turned cold and clammy. The therapist asked me if I was okay... I told her I was fine, I just had some gas underneath my chest cavity. She mentioned how pale I looked and said she needed to take me to the emergency room. I told her I would be fine, however, the next thing I knew, I found myself on the table in the emergency room. I passed out twice before she could get me there. They said I was having a heart attack!

So here I was, once again, back in the hospital for another two weeks. I was thinking, *Okay, enough is enough! I have had about all I can stand! Something has to give!* My thoughts were, *If I do not get out of this hospital, they are going to kill me!*

At this point, I was more than angry with my deceased husband, I was downright furious! All these questions were flooding my mind: *Why did you leave me when I needed you the most, especially when I was there with you every time you were sick? Why was God allowing all these trials and tribulations to come upon me? Why must I be the one to deal with all this chaos?* I was actually thinking, *So what if I died, I will be in a better place, I will not be sick anymore! I will be free from all sorrow and all pain!* I even prayed, *Lord, just please take me home!* Now, I am sure that you have never done anything like that or have you? However, of course, He did not, because He was not through with me, yet! In addition, He is not through with you, either!

I was angry and full of self-pity. Everything was about me at that moment. This was surely a full-blown case of the spirit of heaviness. Mourning, grief, and sorrow had flooded my life. The spirit of heaviness was a stronghold in my life brought on because of my grief and the horrific tragedy I had experienced. The way I found my husband and the look on his face had been etched in my memory. There were times when I would even be praising and worshipping God, when all of a sudden his face would flash before me. It was almost like a jolt of electricity flowing through me!

In facing loneliness, desperation, depression, broken-heartedness, and financial disaster, I found that my only source was God. He was the only one who could fix what was wrong with me. God-given grief is for us to release our pain and our sorrow but, like everything else, Satan has a counterfeit for it. When it turns to self-pity and depression, it only serves to keep us bound. God meant it for good and for our freedom. Grief and mourning are to help us release our hurts and sorrows, not to hold on to them.

We tend to hash and rehash what happened. Picture this: the definition for hash is to chop or cut up into tiny pieces. That is exactly what it does to us each time we relive the incident, whether it was an accident, sickness, suicide, or murder. None of those things holds good memories for us, therefore, we need to put them in the past and leave them there.

We begin to identify ourselves with the tragedy, but God wants us to have our identity in Him. Our identity should come from who we are or who God says we are, in Christ Jesus.

Our focus must be directly toward God, first. Second, we should channel our focus to the good times we had with the person or persons we lost. He told us:

> Finally, brethren, whatsoever things are true, whatsoever things are honest, whatsoever things are just, whatsoever things are pure, whatsoever things are lovely, whatsoever things are of good report, if there be any virtue and if there be any praise, think on these things.
>
> Philippians 4:8 (KJV)

When we are able to think on the good and the godly things, then we are able to move on to the next phase of our lives. I challenge you to get out of the pit of self-pity! Paul said it like this:

> But this one thing I do, forgetting those things which are behind, and reaching forth unto those things which are before, I press toward the mark for the prize of the high calling of God in Christ Jesus.
>
> Philippians 3:13-14 (KJV)

While I was in the hospital this time, they did various tests. The doctor said they found a blockage that needed immediate surgery. He was in the process of arranging for me to be in another state the next morning. The doctor did his best to convince me to have this procedure. He informed me that I would not survive without this surgery.

I just did not have peace about that situation. I just flat out told him, I had to go home and talk to my Father, first. He thought I meant my earthly father, but I was speaking of my heavenly Father.

When he left the room, I started to weep and pray. I asked my Father in heaven what I should do. My husband's Bible was on the bed beside me, and I felt impressed to pick it up. As I laid it in my lap, it opened to the passage in Ezekiel, to the passage that is so dear to my heart. In that particular Bible, certain scriptures are in large script letters across the page. This scripture was in that manner. The scripture read:

> And I will give you a new heart and put a new Spirit within you; I will take the heart of stone out of your flesh and give you a heart of flesh. I will put My Spirit within you and cause you to walk in My statutes, and you will keep My judgments and do them.
>
> Ezekiel 36:26-27 (NKJV)

Perhaps, now you can understand why that portion of scripture is so precious to me. Not only did God give me a new spiritual heart, a heart that had been hard now became soft, pliable, and tender, but He also gave me a new physical heart as an added bonus. He always does more than we expect or ask Him to do.

The oil of joy for mourning and a garment of praise for the spirit of heaviness began to overflow within me. I made my decision. Surgery, absolutely not! I did not need anything else to convince me that God was definitely on my side. Would you not agree? After all, it would be painless if God healed me. There would not be any medical bills or loss of work. It sounded just like God to me!

The most difficult challenge was yet to come, and that was how to convince my family. Naturally, they only wanted what was best for me, whatever would keep me alive the longest. The battle was on but, as I said before, God was on my side. "What then shall we say to these things? If God be for us, who can be against us" (Romans 8:31, KJV).

To date, I have not had any kind of heart surgery. Yes, there have been times when severe pain and discomfort would strike. In those times, I prayed, and others prayed with and for me. I would rebuke the heart attack, which usually comes from a spirit of fear. Shortly thereafter, the pain and discomfort would subside. We must totally surrender ourselves to the Lord and in that surrender, the power or the anointing comes in to overcome and be victorious over any situation.

The enemy wants to keep us beaten down and discouraged. It is the lie of the enemy that causes us to believe we cannot get out of a bad situation. Remember, his assignment is to steal, kill, and destroy. Please, keep this truth close to your heart: anything Satan tells you is a lie from the pit of hell. The truth is not in him. Therefore, in any given situation, the opposite is true from what Satan is saying!

Satan was a murderer, a liar, and a thief from the very beginning. Therefore, he cannot stand in the truth, because there is no truth found in him. When he speaks a lie, he speaks from his own resources, for he is a liar and the father of it.

John 8:44 (NKJV)

Did you get that? There is absolutely no truth in him. The truth is only in what God says about you!

The year after my husband died, I truly believe Satan did everything he could possibly do to kill me, literally. In that year, I was in the hospital more than in my entire life. First, it was my back and then my heart. Next, I went into the hospital for a blood clot in my leg, which disappeared after prayer. My last hospitalization was for bronchial pneumonia and asthma, which I am still battling today. However, I am not defeated; I am still standing on the word of God that says I am healed!

One day, I was praying and pruning flowers at the same time. I pray a lot when I am driving or just doing ordinary things. As I was pruning the flowers, God spoke to my heart; I heard Him so clearly. He said, "This is what I'm doing to you. I am pruning you. I am cutting off some things in the natural and in the spiritual realm. I'm cutting relationships, resources, and anything that you are dependent upon, other than Me." He asked, "Why are you cutting off the branches, even though they look healthy?" My response was so there would be new growth, so it would become fuller. He said, "That's why I am pruning you; there will be new growth and more fruit." Let me tell you, He did exactly what He said He was going to do. He pruned me so much that I wondered if I would survive! I had to be totally dependent upon God. A word to the wise, humble yourself and place your total dependency upon God before He humbles you!

QUESTIONS FOR REFLECTION

Are you encountering abnormal periods of pain, sorrow, grief, mourning, loneliness, depression, desperation, anxiety, or fear?

Are you in self-pity?

Have you gone through episodes of isolation, shutting yourself off from everyone and everything?

Have you lost interest in the things in which you were interested?

What are your eating and sleeping patterns like, have they changed?

Do you find yourself believing the lies of the enemy?

Have you lost your identity of who you are in Christ?

Could you have a spirit of heaviness?

Have you been pruned by God, lately?

What has God extracted from your life and why?

PRAYER

Father,
In the name of Jesus, You have given us power and authority over every demonic force, which tries to kill, steal, and destroy. We bind up all death, destruction, and theft. All incidents and accidents are bound, along with all poverty and lack, all sickness, disease, infirmity and pestilence. We bind up all evil or negative works and forbid them to have any adverse affects in our lives. We bind every trap, snare and plan of the enemy so it cannot work. We declare that no weapon formed against

us shall prosper. Now that all these things are bound up, we cast them from us and sever their ties to us. We do not want them any longer and refuse to take them back. These works of evil are sent back to the pits of hell and are utterly, destroyed by the Word, the Blood, and the name of Jesus Christ. Father, I ask that You fill me with Your precious Holy Spirit, with the Fruit of the Spirit, and the Gifts of the Spirit. Fill me up, Lord, so there is no room for any form of evil to slip back in. Help me to draw closer to You than I have ever been. Cause me to hunger and thirst after Your righteousness. Give me beauty for ashes, the oil of joy for mourning, the garment of praise for the spirit of heaviness. The spirit of heaviness no longer has control over me in the name of Jesus. I declare that the joy of the Lord is my strength. When I go through the pruning process, help me not to resist or fight back; but to be humble. I ask that you make it as painless as possible. These things I pray in the name of Jesus. Amen.

New Beginnings

*I*s it not ironic how this chapter turned out? In case you have not noticed, this is the eighth chapter of the book! This was not in my plans from the beginning of the book, I assure you. Numbers in the Bible have specific meanings. The number eight represents a new beginning. For instance, how many people were on the ark? There were eight: Noah and his wife, their three sons, Shem, Ham, Japheth, and their wives. They were the only ones left alive. There was to be a new beginning in the Earth, a whole new generation.

God gave me a completely new beginning. First, there came the pruning, which was not pleasant. God removed everything from my life, which stunted, stopped or hindered my growth in Him. Next, came the preparation.

Preparation time is a season, where you are set aside. God is grooming you, just as He did with Esther in the book of Esther. God was preparing her for her destiny, her purpose, her calling, and for the King. God was preparing me, "for such a time as this!" He is preparing me for His kingdom, His plans, and His purpose. He is also preparing me as His bride.

The sooner you realize He is doing the same for you, the sooner you can resume your life and be the woman God called you to be. Stop struggling with the plans God has for you or you will drown yourself in self-pity, grief, or sorrow. It is like a swimmer who is drowning; if he struggles against the rescuer, they both may drown. It could be the death of your dreams and visions, the death of the plans God has for you. If worse comes to worse, it could even mean a physical or spiritual death. Just put yourself in the arms of God, your rescuer, and trust Him with the plans He has for your life. Read Jeremiah 29:11, and memorize it. Keep it close to your heart.

After my husband died, I had to move for several different reasons. I believe, most of all, that God was giving me a new start. Remember, the number eight means a new beginning. Get this; my new address was 404 8th Street. I counted this as a double new beginning. Even though it did not look like it in the natural with all the sickness, I counted it a blessing.

During this time of preparation, I spent a great deal of time alone with God. I watched Christian programming in the morning before I left for work. Evenings, I would pray, read the word of God, and other books about the Word. I prayed and sought the counsel of the Holy Spirit about the books I would read. I think this is very important, because there are a tremendous number of books out there that might only serve to confuse you.

This is an example of the statement I just made. I received a letter in the mail the other day and upon opening it, I began to read about the secrets to an abundant life. It spoke about possessing the desires of your heart. She mentioned success, prosperity, and it even brought God into it. It all sounded so good at the beginning that it nearly lulls your discernment to sleep. Then it started talking about a secret society, and the secrets of that society. This woman gave her personal testimony about all the things this society had done for her, and how it had changed her life. She spoke of having the ability to read the minds of others, and could actually predict what they would do. She spoke about being able to do things in art and music that she could not do before. By this time, I am thinking, *What in the world have I opened myself up to?* She then made the statement she had lost weight and started looking more beautiful.

She mentioned that her husband was much more enchanted by her; but the thing that really quickened my spirit was the fact that she stated other men desired to have a relationship with her, also. She was even giving God praise for these things.

Sometimes, I am a little naïve! Now, I am wondering what god she is talking about, because it sure is not the God I serve. I decided; I did not need to read further. I covered myself with the Blood of Jesus and asked for His protection, so that the door I had opened would be shut and sealed by the blood. When my husband came home, I told him about the letter and asked him to agree with me in prayer over it. Immediately after we prayed, I took the letter to the trash and burned it.

Ladies, just a word of warning, be careful what you open up yourself to. It could be as innocent as opening the mail. If something similar should happen to you, repent and ask for the protection of the Blood of Jesus.

Anyway, back to the preparation time. During the preparation, for the most part, my television was off. At this particular time, I was watching a lot of Christian television, until the Lord spoke to my heart and told me He was jealous of my time. Even though my television viewing was programs about God, it interfered with my intimate time with Him. I watched Christian programming in the morning, before work, for encouragement. Other than that, the television was silent for approximately a year.

During this time, I did a lot of soul searching. I sought the Lord like never before. I read books that would inspire, encourage, and lift me up; books that helped strengthen my faith. I prayed for a supernatural anointing of faith. I craved the promises of God, because I needed something to hold on to, desperately!

Someone that inspired me immensely was Michelle McKinney Hammond. If you have not read one of her books, you really should take the time to invest in yourself through her ministry. She is a spectacular woman of God and powerfully anointed. She will inspire and lift you up, especially if you are a single woman and/or have a low self-worth. At that time, I was still a widow without a lot of self-confidence.

She taught me a great deal about how you are to be treated and how you are to treat yourself. Furthermore, she wrote concerning the qualities to search for in a godly husband, and what qualities a godly man is searching for in a wife. She will make you laugh and cry, but you will be a better all-around person after reading her books. I recommend reading them to anyone, especially a single woman. The bottom line is that all women could benefit from her writings. I have derived so much wisdom from her works, that there have been times when I bought her books and gave them away for ministry.

After studying the Bible and reading several books of encouragement, I began to believe in myself again. Realizing who I was in God and who God said I was, I began to have more self-confidence, which I gained from God and His Word and other ministries. My walk began to have more bounce and energy in it. There was definitely something different about my countenance, and my smile returned. When you know who you are in God, things begin to change rapidly. I cannot explain it, but I began to attract the positive things life had to offer instead of the negative. It seemed as though people became attracted to the positive aspect within me. If you are positive, you will attract positive people and things. If you are negative, you will attract the negative. Have you ever heard misery loves company? Well, there is more truth to that statement than you can imagine!

There is an opinion that when you get to the point where you are content to be with God, and only God, and should you desire to have a spouse, God will send him. That is exactly what happened to me. I reached the point where I was content with God. I wanted only the person who God desired for me to have as a spouse. My advice to you: make God your husband before you seek a husband of flesh. Seek the spiritual first, and then the natural will come. "But seek ye first, the Kingdom of God, and His righteousness; and all these things shall be added unto you" (Matthew 6:33, KJV).

Yes, there were many times when I was lonely. There were many times, when I just needed someone to talk to, someone tangible. Someone with whom I could share the everyday cares of life, my hopes, and my dreams. There were other times when I just needed the comfort and security of a husband beside me. However, more than that, I wanted the one that God was preparing me for, and the one God was preparing for me. If you are still waiting for that special person, do not be disheartened. It is not that God has denied your prayers or your desires. He is not finished with His preparation of you, your spouse, or both of you. The quicker you get in tune with God's pruning, preparation, and His divine plan for your life, the quicker those desires will manifest.

Preparation time varies. Mainly, it depends upon your submission to God. My preparation went on nearly three years. What can I say; I guess I am a slow learner! It only took a year for Esther! During my time with the Lord, He told me to write down exactly what I wanted in a husband.

> And the Lord answered me and said: "Write the vision and make it plain upon tablets, that he may run that readeth it. For the vision is yet for an appointed time, but at the end it shall speak, and not lie: though it tarry, wait for it; because it will surely come, it will not tarry."
> Habakkuk 2:2-3 (KJV)

This scripture in Habakkuk explains why it is so important to write down your hopes, dreams, and goals for your life. You are supposed to write them down on paper and on the tablets of your heart. You write it down and then, if it lines up with the word of God, God will bring it to pass.

My list was quite lengthy. There were several specific things, I requested in a husband. I prayed concerning the desires of my heart, in order that his desires would be in line with mine. I also prayed our desires would be in alignment with God's desires. In this way, we would be equally yoked together. Remember, I wrote how important and biblical it is to be yoked equally. At the risk of sounding "corny," my list consisted of the following:

1. Above all, he will love God with all his heart, body, spirit, soul, and with all of his substance. He would hunger and thirst for God.

2. He will love me as Christ loves the church, willing to lay down his life for me.

3. My best friend and my lover.

4. A heart for ministry.

5. Loving, compassionate, passionate, tender, kind, and trustworthy.

6. Filled with the Holy Spirit of God.

7. The fruit of the Spirit will be evident in his life.

8. A heart for giving in every area of his life.

9. Blessed exceedingly, abundantly above all he could ask or think.

10. A good listener and a respecter of my opinions.

11. He will love my family, my children, and my grandchildren.

12. He will nurture me and help me to grow.

13. He will celebrate me, not just tolerate me.

14. A godly husband, father, and grandfather.

15. Attractive spiritually and physically.

16. Beautiful eyes that reflect what is truly in his spirit.

17. Where I am weak, he will be strong. Where he is weak, I will be strong. I will be his missing rib!

18. Both of us will give 100 percent to God, marriage, family, and ministry.

19. Filled with wisdom, knowledge, and understanding.

20. A good steward of what God has given him.

21. Most importantly, handpicked and sent by God!

Step out on faith, comprise your own list, but only after much prayer and a lot of soul searching. Some of the above requests may seem to overlap each other, but I wanted to make sure all the bases were covered. A word of caution: Be specific and be careful what you ask for; you may just get it!

Stepping out on faith may prove to be difficult. Take small steps, like making your list. I made a list, and then I began to buy things for the bedroom. I even began to set the table, as if my spouse was already there. Make sure your thoughts, your words, and your actions line up with the things you desire from God.

If it seems like nothing is happening, just hold on to the promises of God. His promises are "Yes" and "Amen." Only God knows how, when, and where he will come into your life, so do not give up hope. Just continue to do the things you know to do, leave the rest up to God.

A word to the wise, ladies, my husband also had a list. Spend your time alone with God, preparing yourself for destiny and your husband.

People tried to set me up with dates. My first question to them was, "Is he a Christian?" Usually they were not Christians; therefore, my answer would be, "No, thank you." Co-workers would talk to me about going different places to meet men, such as Christian single groups. I told them I would feel like I was going to a meat market. I knew in my heart, that was not where I would meet my future husband. There is not anything wrong in participating in Christian singles groups, it just was not right for me. I did date one person who attended the same church as I did; but he did not celebrate me in the way a daughter of the King should be celebrated. A word of warning: If those who are in spiritual authority over you caution you concerning that person or relationship, it would be to your advantage to listen intently! Many times, they are able to see more clearly, because they are not affected by emotional deafness and blindness.

An evangelist, Jerry Baldree, spoke a prophecy over me at a church revival service. There were two things prevalent in my heart that night: my son and my future spouse. The prophecy was that the answer to my prayers would walk through the door of my office and sit down beside me. Immediately, I thought the Spirit was talking about my son's release from prison.

Later that year, I received another prophecy from a different prophet, stating that my future husband had been watching me from a distance. A year prior to this, I attended a class at our church. I met a man named Tom, whose wife had left him several months earlier. Our whole group, myself included, prayed for him and his wife to be reunited. They did get back together for a short time, but she left again a few months later.

Tom was in construction and had a contract to work on my father-in-law's house. They became close, so my father-in-law invited him to our church home group. Little did he know; Tom and I had already met approximately a year prior. Tom was surprised to see me there. I will never forget the look on his face when he said, "What are you doing here?"

I returned with a quick response, "What are you doing here? I have been meeting with this home group for over three years!"

One day, unexpectedly, he walked into my office and plopped himself down in the chair beside my desk. At first, I thought this could not be of God; this must be a test. I had an extremely hard struggle within my heart as to whether or not I could trust him, or any man, for that matter! While I was praying, the Lord spoke to me, saying, "I did not call you to trust man; I called you to trust

Me." Well, that more or less settled it in my spirit. It was not long before Tom won my trust.

The Bible says, "He who finds a wife finds a good thing, and obtains favor from the Lord" (Proverbs 18:22, NKJV). Ladies, please take special note of this statement. The man finds the wife, not the wife finds the husband. He is supposed to be the one who does the pursuing. Most women today have this liberated idea that it is okay to pursue the man, myself included, at one time. The man likes the challenge of pursuit. Be approachable, but not easily persuaded!

Tom is now my husband. We married on August 8th; please notice it is the eighth month, eighth day. For us, that date meant another double new beginning. What a godsend he is to me! He found me, pursued me, and captured my heart.

May I tell you that the list has paid off? I tease Tom all the time, telling him that he fulfilled 90 percent of the list. Then I proceed to tell him that God and I are still working on the other 10 percent!

A word of wisdom: If you are not married, but you are in a relationship where you are doing the pursuing, instead of the other way around, break it off! If he does not celebrate you, break it off! If he is not a godly man, break it off!

My husband, Tom, truly celebrates me. He has a heart as big as they come. He treats my family, children, and grandchildren with great love and respect. Tom's family graciously accepted my family as an extension of their family. Tom has four children, Tom, Jr., Chris, Libby, and Jennifer. Also included are two sons-in-law, David and Barry. He also has two grandchildren, Andrew and Hannah. They have all become very dear to my heart. These two families are not just his family or my family; they have become our family. What a wonderful blessing!

Mothers, if you find yourself in a situation of starting over, please consider your children. Your happiness and the entire extended family are at stake when such a change takes place. They have to make drastic changes in their lives, also. Have godly compassion for them during this time of transition. You cannot expect your family to love that person the way you do, in the beginning. They have to earn the love, trust, and respect of those family members. Remember, they have many trust issues they have to resolve, especially if they are older and there have been multiple partners running in and out of their lives. On the other hand, if they or their parent has been mistreated or abused in previous relationships. Younger children do not have preconceived notions; they love unconditionally. Their only desire is for love in return. Tom and I thank God for the family we have; though it is a blended family, it is a blessed family!

Now, I am not insinuating we have a perfect marriage, because we do not. In fact, I do not know of one couple, who does. There will be only one perfect marriage that consists of Jesus Christ and His bride, which is the Church! I do know, however, without a shadow of doubt, that God Himself orchestrated our marriage. Remember the prophecies; they did not cross my mind, again, until months after we were married. It really blew my mind! God is so awesome!

We both have a heart for ministry. Right now, we are in the process of starting the ministry for which God has given us the vision. We have named it Harvest Ministries. The original vision started with Tom long before we ever met; but now our ministries and visions have become one.

Naturally, this is a process, just the same as becoming one in a marriage is a process. You are far from being one when you say, "I do." It takes time, a lot of give and take, and a tremendous amount of dying to self. Do not be discouraged; before long, you will be able to finish each other's sentences. You can know what your spouse is thinking just by looking in their eyes.

Our ministry will consist of evangelistic street ministry, dealing with salvation, healing, and deliverance. Please remember us in your prayer time, and lift this ministry up before the Lord. The vision is much greater than we could ever accomplish without God. But then again, if we could accomplish this feat on our own, it would not be God!

QUESTIONS FOR REFLECTION

Are you moving with the flow of God or are
you struggling against the current?

Do you desire a new beginning?

Is God first in your life?

Which do you attract, the negative or the positive?

In what ways do you encourage yourself?

Do you occupy your time with the
things of God or of the world?

God is preparing you for something, what is it?

What qualities and virtues do you desire in a spouse?

Have you written your requests and prayed over them?

If you are in a relationship, does he celebrate you or tolerate you?

Are you pursuing him or is he pursuing you?

Have you prepared yourself and your home for the promise?

PRAYER

Father,
I pray I will be humble and not struggle against the plans
You have designed for me. I do desire a fresh new beginning.
Give me insight as to who I am in Christ. I will do my best
to make You Lord of my life. I will seek You first in all things.
Help me to fill my spirit with things that are godly, uplifting,
encouraging, and positive. Reveal my purpose, destiny and
calling to me. Guide me as I endeavor to list the qualities I

would like in my spouse. If I am in an abusive relationship, give me wisdom, knowledge, and understanding in what I should do. If I am in a relationship, where I am not celebrated and I am married then I ask You to change it; but if my spouse is unwilling to change, reveal to me what I am to do according to Your will. If I am not married then dissolve the relationship. Send someone who will celebrate, pursue and complete me. Lord, please prepare me for the promises, You have in store, and help me to prepare my home and myself. All these things I ask in the name of Jesus. Amen.

Desires of Your Heart

If you are a woman after God's own heart, then you are truly a "lady in waiting." The desires you have are God-given desires. In other words, they are desires God placed on the inside of your heart. Your calling and purpose in life are directly connected to your desires. Let me reiterate, whatever moves you, makes you cry or makes you angry, that is your passion.

What exactly is a desire? To desire something or someone means to wish for, to want, to crave, or a longing. God said in His Word He would give us the desires of our hearts. "Delight thyself also in the Lord, and He shall give thee the desires of thine heart" (Psalm 37:4, KJV).

Do you know what it means to delight in the Lord? This means you totally submit to His perfect will for your life. You commit everything to Him, completely, not withholding anything. You will want to know Him better and more intimately. You receive joy from spending time with someone you love, especially when they love you in return. You cannot truly love someone if you do not share time with him or her. The more time spent together, the more you know that person, and the more you can love them. You cannot know or understand God's ways if you do not spend time alone with His Word and in communion with Him.

After all, He knows the beginning from the end, and He knows us better than we know ourselves. If we want what is best for us, "Father knows best!" Put your trust in Him, implicitly! Trust Him with everything that concerns you. That means your spouse, children, health, finances, job, or career; in every area of your life, turn it over to His hands.

Let me ask you a question, when you buy a house, do you purchase every room in the house? On the other hand, does the seller of the house tell you that every room in the house belongs to you, except one room? Of course not, there are no exclusions when you buy a house. All the rooms belong to the buyer.

Now consider this. Jesus Christ purchased you on the cross—if you are a believer. Therefore, every part of your being and every part of your life belongs solely to Him. He paid the ultimate price for you. Do not withhold any part of your life from Him.

Open every door in your heart, especially the doors to the darkest, coldest, innermost chambers. We all have areas where we have hidden things, terrible hurts, and scars of life, places where we do not dwell very long ourselves, much less let anyone else enter, because it is so painful.

Listen carefully! The absolute, only way the pain, hurt or, perhaps, shame, ever dissipates, is to open up to Jesus Christ. Allow His light and love to enter into the darkness. Where there is light, the darkness has to flee. As the light and love, Who is Jesus Christ, enters in, healing will come.

Once you have accomplished this, God can do marvelous works in your life and those around you. However, as long as you try to handle it on your own, the Lord will let you have your way. He will not take it out of your hands; you have to give it to Him. Why not give Him your all; He already knows everything anyway.

In the past, I have turned certain areas of my life over to God, then immediately took them back. Do not do as I have done. Once you give it to Him, leave it there!

"Lord, all my desire is before You; (or known to You) And my sighing is not hidden from You" (Psalm 38:9, NKJV). In other words, He knows exactly what we long for; He knows every word we speak and every thought we think. God knows what we need before we ask. What an awesome God we serve!

Delight yourself in the Lord, surrender to Him, let Him have full reign in your life; then, and only then, will He be able to give you the desires of your heart!

QUESTIONS FOR REFLECTION

Are you indeed a woman after God's Own heart?

What are your innermost desires?

What makes you cry?

What makes you angry or sad?

What moves you and what is your passion?

Do you know Jesus Christ, intimately?

Have you excluded Him from any area of your life, including your deepest, darkest secrets?

PRAYER

Father,

I sincerely want to be a woman after Your Own heart. My desire is to know You more intimately. I surrender my all to You, even the things I have not shared with anyone else. Give me the strength and the courage so I will not withhold anything from You. I thank you for the Godly desires you have place within me. Show me how to implement action with my passion. Give me the heart of God and the mind of

Christ. Anoint my eyes to see spiritually so that I see what You see. Anoint my ears to hear Your voice clearly and help me to obey without hesitation. Shield me from the voice of the flesh or the voice of the enemy. Anoint my tongue so that I will use it for healing, edification, encouragement, and ministry. I will speak life and not death; blessings instead of curses; positive and not negative. Anoint my hands and use them as an extension of Your hands. Anoint my feet to walk in the paths of righteousness, to stay on the path You have mapped out for me; and to run to do Your will. All these requests I ask in the name of Jesus. So be it unto me. Amen.

Pearl of Great Price
and Beauty

$\mathcal{F}$irst, let me say, I am very thankful to God that I was born in the United States of America. If you are privileged enough to live here, you are blessed beyond measure. Some countries treat women as possessions, not treasures. Now, I realize there are exceptions to every rule. Due to the fact, I have been an exception at different intervals of my life.

When you or someone else makes you feel you are not worthy, remember that Jesus Christ counted you worthy of all His suffering before, during, and after the cross. If you had been the only one, He would have given His life freely, just for you. That reveals to me exactly how much you and I are worth. He laid down everything for us. Jesus Christ considered women as precious to Him as any man. He paid the same price for women as He paid for men. Jesus treated women with love, honor, dignity, and respect. He is no respecter of persons! "Then Peter replied, 'I see very clearly that God doesn't show partiality' (Acts 10:34, NLT).

Many women were used mightily in the word of God and throughout the ages. Women are being used increasingly more in ministry today, and it will continue to increase with each passing day.

If you are on this earth, God has a purpose and a destiny for you in His kingdom. It may not be in the church sphere; it may be in the marketplace. The Holy Spirit will reveal His purpose for your life, if you first seek the kingdom of God.

Included in the Bible were women like Mary, the mother of Jesus, who was used as a young teenager to birth, nurture, and teach our Messiah. She trusted God with her very life, because women in that day were stoned if they were found with child and unmarried. Therefore, if you are a young "lady in waiting," you are definitely not off the hook. In fact, the time to start serving God, accept the Lord Jesus Christ, as your Savior, and to be filled with the Holy Spirit, is at a very early and tender age. You could save yourself a great deal of heartache and pain if you commit yourself to the Lord, totally and completely.

God used Naomi and Ruth, both widows, who were in the lineage of Jesus. Some of you feel you do not have much self-worth, because there is not a man or a husband in your life. That could not be further from the truth. You are a marvelous, glorious, one of a kind, and unique creation of God. God can use you and bring your spouse in the process, if you allow Him to work in your life.

God used women, from whom Jesus had cast out demons. Mary Magdalene was such a woman; but she was also the first person to whom Jesus appeared after His resurrection from the tomb. He used adulterers, divorcees, and even the demon-possessed!

Rahab was used by God to protect the two spies, and helped them escape death. Because of this service for the kingdom of God, she and her household were saved when all the people in the city where she lived were destroyed. In Joshua 2, there is an account of their salvation. The spies told her to leave the scarlet rope hanging from the window of her house, and everyone inside would be saved. The scarlet rope was a representation of the blood of Jesus Christ. Rahab was a harlot; but she was also in the lineage of Jesus, and considered a daughter of great faith!

Deborah was a great leader, a judge over Israel, a songwriter, and a prophetess. She knew how to handle people and circumstances. Deborah was a very wise woman. She was willing, obedient, and careful to give God the glory; therefore, God used her mightily.

Anna, the prophetess, lived in the temple where Jesus was dedicated to God eight days after His birth. Anna moved into the temple when she became a widow, just seven years after she married. She was now a mature woman of eight-four years old. She dedicated her life to prayer, fasting, and worship of God, day and night; while she waited for the promised Messiah. Anna was truly a "lady in waiting" for the promises of God. Anna portrayed great endurance. She recognized Jesus as Lord and Savior, and testified to everyone about Jesus, the promised King.

Dorcas, who was also called Tabitha, performed many charitable acts for the people in her community, especially the widows and the poor. You may be called just to your family, church, or community, to do good unto those that are less fortunate than you are. If this is your calling, do not belittle the call. It is just as important as any other calling. Be obedient, for God recognizes this as success. God blesses us, so we may be a blessing to others. When God shows you a person in need, do everything in your power to meet that need.

> Do not withhold good from those who deserve it when it's in your power to help them. If you can help your neighbor now, don't say, "Come back tomorrow and then I'll help you."
> Proverbs 3:27-28 (NLT)

In the book of Esther, it tells us that Esther was prepared for a year before she was presented and then chosen as the king's wife. Often while we wait, God is preparing something spectacular for us. Sometimes, we are left in a state of limbo while we continue to wait, not knowing the things God has prepared. "No eye has seen, no ear has heard, and no mind has imagined what God has prepared for those who love Him" (1 Corinthians 2:9, NLT). It is in this time we have to trust God completely, holding on to our faith without wavering. Seek out the things God has prepared for you.

Unselfishly, Esther put her life in jeopardy so that she could help deliver the Jewish nation. God honored and rewarded her by giving her the desires of her heart. The word of God says that Esther was set apart for such a time as this! Why have you been set apart? Remember, if you honor God with your obedience; He will honor you in due season.

Elizabeth, Hannah, Rachel, and Sarah were all barren. In biblical days, a woman who was barren was considered cursed. Through God's mercy and grace, He shined upon these "ladies in waiting." They each had waited a very long time for the promise of a child.

God blessed Elizabeth by giving her a son in her old age. This child turned out to be John the Baptist, the forerunner of Jesus Christ. His message was of repentance and the coming Messiah. Elizabeth waited many years for her promise. Greatness will always come to those that wait upon the Lord.

God blessed Hannah when she conceived a son. After many years of being barren, Hannah promised God that she would dedicate her firstborn son, Samuel, to the Lord by handing him over to Eli, the priest.

I cannot imagine giving up one of my children, can you? I realize many mothers have suffered the loss of a child through tragedy. What a horrifying and heart-wrenching experience this must be! My brother and his wife lost a son at approximately three months old; it must have been unbelievably painful for them and their other son. It is so very difficult to know what to say when something like this happens.

Through all of this, God honored Hannah by giving her other children. Samuel was called by God to be the greatest judge over Israel, a prophet, and a priest.

Rachel also proved to be a "lady in waiting" for her husband and, later, for her children. She waited for seven years for Jacob to work out the agreement he made with her father, in order that they could be married. Her father, Laban, deceived them both. On what was to be their wedding night, Laban sent Leah, his eldest daughter, to Jacob, instead of Rachel. The custom of the day was the eldest daughter had to be married before the younger. Therefore, Rachel and Jacob had to wait another week before they could marry. In addition, Jacob had to work another seven years for Rachel. She stood on the promise, as she watched her sister birth children year after year. God looked upon her affliction and gave her two sons. Joseph, her firstborn, later saved his entire family from starvation and extinction.

Last, but not least, Sarah was also a "lady in waiting" for a long period. Sarah's mistake was the fact that she did not wait quite long enough! She decided; she was too old for God to give her children; so, she took matters into her own hands. Sarah devised a plan where Abraham would go to her servant and she would conceive, therefore giving them a son. However, that was not God's plan! When we try to help God or when we give up on the promises of God, we can get into serious trouble. After all, would you rather have the promise of the flesh or the promise of the Spirit?

Ishmael was a child of the flesh, but Isaac was a child of the Spirit. Getting ahead of God will cause division and destruction. In all of this, the Word still says Sarah was a woman of faith; she became the mother of a nation and an ancestor of Jesus.

Even through our messes, our failures, shortcomings, and our lack of self-worth, God is not limited. Jesus Christ is still faithful and just, to forgive us and to redeem us from our past, present, and our future!

As you can see, God used homemakers, adulterers, prostitutes, women that were barren, and women of all different marital statuses. He chose those who, by the world's standards, were cursed! God uses women from all walks of life, all shapes, sizes, nationalities, ages, and even faiths. You see, what you have done, where you have been, what circumstances or situations you are in or have been through, it does not matter to God. It does not matter if you are young or old, rich or poor, sick or healthy, single, married, divorced, or widowed. It does not matter to Him if you are a genius or not! God has a place for you in His kingdom, and it is a place only you can fill. Most importantly, there is also a place in your heart, which can only be filled by Him. Nothing or no one else will ever be able to fill that void in your life.

We have looked at the way Jesus sees us and how He treats us. He did not condemn, but instead laid down His life, because He loved us so much. Now let us evaluate how we are supposed to be treated by the men in our lives.

It plainly states in the word of God that the husband is supposed to love us, as Christ loved the Church, and be willing to lay down his life for her. Christ is the husband of the Church, and the Church is the bride of Christ. A marriage between a husband and wife should reflect the same kind of love.

I know you probably do not want to hear this; but here it is, anyway. The Word also tells us to be submissive to our husband, to honor and respect him. For the husband, the Word tells him to love his wife. If a man loves his wife, he will govern their marriage in love and not as a dictator or a tyrant! If a man loves his wife, it will be easy for her to be submissive to him, because she knows he will ultimately do what is best for her. If you know someone truly loves you, would you not agree that it is easy to trust him or her?

> For a husband is the head of his wife as Christ is the head of His body, the church; He gave His life to be her Savior. As the church submits to Christ, so you wives must submit to your husbands in everything. And you husbands must love your wives with the same love Christ showed the church. He gave up His life for her.
>
> Ephesians 5:23-25 (NLT)

I would like to add one other thing. You are to be submissive in all things, unless it does not line up with the word of God. Remember, the Word is your guideline!

> Likewise, you husbands, dwell with them with understanding, giving honor to the wife, as to the weaker vessel, and as being together in the grace of life, that your prayers may not be hindered.
>
> 1 Peter 3:7 (NLT)

This is a powerful statement. God says it is so important to Him to protect you, that if your husband is not obedient in the way he cares for you, his prayers will be hindered!

In conclusion, your husband should love you, honor, and understand you. Now, ladies, you know as well as I do, there is absolutely no way he could understand you at all times, because we do not understand ourselves at all times. My point is, he should at least be in tune with God, and try to understand. He should protect you, even to the point of laying down his life for you. Ladies, how can you not love, honor, respect and, yes, even submit to a man like that? I can hear you now, loud and clear, "My husband is not such a man!" My answer to you is: "Pray, pray, pray for your spouse to become the man God wants him to be, then he will become the man you want him to be." A little advice here, pray first that God will change you. It may take a while, but God will honor a prayer like that.

> Again, the kingdom of heaven is like unto a merchant man, seeking goodly pearls, who, when he had found one pearl of great price, went and sold all that he had and bought it.
>
> Matthew 13:45-46 (NLT)

I felt the Spirit saying, in relation to women, they are like pearls, pearls of great price and beauty.

If a man truly loves a woman, he will give all to have her. He will give up all the little pearls in his life, for that one special pearl. He will love and honor her enough to marry her. In scripture, it says when a man finds a wife he finds a good thing.

Be that pearl of great price and beauty! Do not be the pearl cast before swine, to be trampled under their feet. You are worth much more than you realize!

> Give not that which is holy unto the dogs, neither cast your pearls before swine, lest they trample them under their feet, and turn again and rend you.
>
> Matthew 7:6 (NLT)

If we are pearls, we need to present ourselves and dress like the pearls that we are. The women of today do not realize the way they dress reflects on Jesus Christ. "In like manner also, these women adorn themselves in modest apparel" (1 Timothy 2:9, NLT). Rest assured, I am not one for clothesline preaching; but the way some women, even Christian women, adorn themselves should be a little more modest. The mature ladies should teach the younger ladies how to dress more appropriately. I am speaking of maturity in relationship to Christ, not age. Let us teach them to be fashionable, but decent! Remember, we should not cause anyone to stumble or fall.

When I was young in age and in the Lord, the ladies in our congregation frowned upon the younger ladies, because they wore pants instead of dresses. I will never forget my pastor preaching to the congregation about this very subject. He corrected the older ladies for their gossiping, backbiting, and condemnation. His statement was this: "If you could see what I see, from where I stand (the pulpit), you would wish more ladies would wear pants." That one statement shut their mouths for good!

Let us present ourselves holy, thus teaching by example with love, not condemnation!

The aged women likewise, that they be in behavior as becometh holiness, not false accusers, not given to much wine, teachers of good things; that they may teach the young women to be sober, to love their husbands, to love their children, to be discreet, chaste, keepers at home, good, obedient to their own husbands, that the word of God be not blasphemed.

Titus 2:3-5 (NLT)

You were bought with a great price! You were bought and paid for with the life and the precious blood of Jesus Christ. Jesus, Himself, counted you worthy!

For God so loved the world that He gave His only begotten Son, so that everyone who believes in Him will not perish but have eternal life.

John 3:16 (NLT)

Because He counted you worthy, you are now the daughter of the King, a joint heir with Jesus Christ, a new creature, God's masterpiece, and God's chosen. In Genesis 1:26-27, we are told that we were made in God's image, mirrored images of God Himself. You should be a reflection of His character. You are a blessed, highly favored "lady in waiting."

It is time to move on from the past and even the present, to the things God has prepared for you. Press through to the destiny God has surely planned for your life.

Are you truly a lady in waiting for the promises of God? As a woman thinks in her heart, so is she. In the first chapter of this book, I wrote about a "change of heart." Now that you have a change of heart, put your stinking thinking aside, by replacing your mind with the mind of Christ. Renew your mind on a daily basis, like daily bread. Change your thinking to what God thinks about you. You are worthy!

Now, stand up straight, shoulders back, head up, wear a smile on your face, put a spring in your step, and change your mind, your attitude, and fight! If you really want the things of God, then you will have to fight for them. This is not the time to let your guard down; this is war! The Word says the violent take it by force. Do not expect Satan, to just hand your desires over to you, especially, if they are godly desires. You will have to wage spiritual warfare. Fear not; keep the faith with your eyes focused on Jesus, and trust that God will fight the battle for you. "The kingdom of heaven suffereth violence and the violent take it by force" Matthew 11:12, KJV).

There are several virtues involved in being a "lady in waiting." In Proverbs 31, it gives an example of a virtuous woman. These are virtues to strive toward; not to be overwhelmed by; it is a process! Proverbs asks the question, "Who can find a virtuous woman?" It states the virtuous woman is worth more than precious rubies, and she will greatly inspire, enrich, and bless the life of her husband and children. I believe, in this passage, we are compared to "wisdom." In fact, as we just read, the Word compares us to the worth of rubies; also, that we bring blessings. In His Word, wisdom is referred to in the same manner as rubies and blessings.

Become a "lady of wisdom." Wisdom is referred to in the female gender, but have you ever wondered, why? This is something for you to chew on, just a little food for thought.

My belief is that God never uses words just to be using them. He always has purpose in the spoken or written Word. Therefore, there must be more to this than meets the natural eye. We know that God has given us great wisdom; even though, sometimes, we fail to tap into the wisdom; which He has so graciously given us. If you lack wisdom, all you have to do is ask for it!

I realize it was Adam who made the decision to give up paradise, dominion over the Earth, and most important of all, his intimate relationship with God. However, the fact is Eve had great influence with Adam!

As godly women, we need to come to the realization we have great influence with the men in our lives. Let me clarify that statement. I am not talking about manipulation and control. The Bible refers to those things as being witchcraft. We are to use wisdom in building our homes, encouraging our husbands and our children in the ways of God. We do not do this by pushing or manipulating, but by loving and praying for them.

My husband, Tom, and I are reading the book of Proverbs. There is a chapter in Proverbs for each day of the month. Tom said he heard if you read Proverbs every day for at least two years, and then apply it to your life, you would become wealthy. We believe this to be true because of the extraordinary amount of wisdom compiled in those pages. The key word here is to apply the principles given in God's Word.

Remember, Proverbs was mostly written by Solomon, the wisest and wealthiest man to live, ever, according to the Bible. Would you like to possess that kind of wisdom? I believe that if you have wisdom, you can be wealthy in every area of your life, not just the financial. Wisdom is yours for the asking. Have you asked God to give you wisdom?

> If any of you lack wisdom, let him ask of God, that giveth to all men (women) liberally, and upbraided not (rebuke); and it shall be given him (her).
>
> James 1:5 (KJV)

> The law of the wise is a fountain of life, to depart from the snares of death.
>
> Proverbs 13:14 (KJV)

> Happy is the person who finds wisdom and gains understanding. For the profit of wisdom is better than silver, and her wages are better than gold. Wisdom is more precious than rubies; nothing you desire can compare with her. She

offers you life in her right hand, and riches and honor in her left. She will guide you down delightful paths; all her ways are satisfying. Wisdom is a tree of life to those who embrace her; happy are those who hold her tightly. By wisdom the Lord founded the earth; by understanding He established the heavens. By His knowledge the deep fountains of the earth burst forth, and the clouds poured down like rain.

Proverbs 3:13-20 (NLT)

Become a "lady of obedience." There is a promise, if we are obedient to the Word of God:

If they obey and serve Him, they shall spend their days in prosperity, and their years in pleasures.

Job 36:11 (KJV)

If ye be willing and obedient, ye shall eat the good of the land.

Isaiah 1:19 KJV)

If we are obedient, God promises eternal life. "But if you do the will of God, you will live forever" (1 John 2:17, NLT). God's Word says obedience is better than sacrifice.

Become a "lady of joy," always rejoicing. Let the joy of the Lord be your strength. Fulfill your joy by asking for your heart's desires in the name of Jesus. "Hitherto have ye asked nothing in My name: ask, and ye shall receive, that your joy may be full" (John 16:24, KJV). You see, right here, Jesus is telling you to ask. Ask in His name; believe that you have received, and then you will receive, if it is in accordance to His will. When your prayers are answered, you will become stronger in your belief of God's Word.

Become a "lady of love," for we are commanded to love. "He that loveth not, knoweth not God: for God is Love" (1 John 4:8, KJV). The two greatest commandments are to love God first, then love one another. In order that we may be partakers with God, we have to love, because God is love. He is the purest form of love.

We also have to love ourselves, because we were marvelously and wonderfully created by God, fashioned by His own hand. "Thou shalt love thy neighbor as thyself" (Leviticus 19:18, KJV). We are also commanded to love and bless our enemies. "But I say, love your enemies! Pray for those who persecute you" (Matthew 5:44, NLT)! Are you a true reflection of God's love toward yourself and others?

The word "love" is used irresponsibly or too liberally in our society today. We tend to "love" everything, from God to people, places, and things. In order to understand the true meaning of love, we have to understand God. The two of the most accurate descriptions of love are found in Corinthians 13, which is commonly called the "chapter of love" and in John 15. Most importantly, the greatest example is Jesus Christ laying down His life, freely, for you and for me!

> This is My commandment, that ye love one another, as I have loved you. Greater love hath no man than this, that a man lay down his life for his friends. Ye are My friends, if ye do whatsoever I command you.
>
> John 15:12-14 (KJV)

Become a "lady of faith," because this lady in waiting will have the faith that will cause her to persevere and to wait patiently for the promises of God. "Now faith is 'the substance of things hoped for, the evidence of things not seen" (Hebrews 11:1, KJV). The whole chapter of Hebrews 11 is about faith, endurance, and receiving the promise. In fact, it tells us, "Without faith, it is impossible to please God" (Hebrews 11:6, KJV).

The Word tells us to walk by faith, not by sight. It also exhorts us to ask in faith without doubting. Jesus said to the woman, with the issue of blood, that her faith made her whole. Recognize the power of faith within yourself.

Become a "lady of humility," and then the grace of God will cover your life like a blanket of protection.

> Yea, all of you be subject one to another, and be clothed with
> humility; for God resisteth the proud and giveth grace to the
> humble. Humble yourselves therefore under the mighty hand
> of God that He may exalt you in due time.
>
> 1 Peter 5:5-6 (KJV)

Do not try to exalt yourself, or you may be brought to shame. In the right season, God will lift you up and set you in a high place. "By humility and the fear of the Lord are riches, and honor, and life" (Proverbs 22:4, KJV). God will never forget the cries of the humble heart.

Become a "lady of patience and perseverance." Obviously, we have to have these two virtues in order to be able to wait for the promises of God. According to the Word, God clearly tells us that we have need of patience, yes, the very thing we are so against praying about for ourselves. "For ye have need of patience, that after ye have done the will of God, ye might receive the promise" (Hebrews 10:36, KJV).

Many have said they do not desire to ask for patience. Nevertheless, the fact is patience and perseverance plays a very important role in our lives. Patience brings in perfection and lacks nothing. You might want to rethink patience!

> Knowing this, that the trying of your faith worketh patience.
> But let patience have her perfect work, that ye may be perfect
> and entire, wanting nothing.
>
> James 1:3-4 (KJV)

Waiting, as I said earlier, has always been the most difficult part for me. Nevertheless, we must put our trust in the Lord and His plans for our lives. We must endure until the promises come forth. We cannot back up one inch, or Satan will try to take that mile! In the word of God, there are over one hundred and fifty references to the words "wait," "waited," and "waiting." Therefore, there must be virtue in our waiting, somewhere!

In closing this chapter, I want you to remember who you are in Christ Jesus. You are a "pearl of great price and beauty!"

Above all, get wisdom and be obedient in every area of your life. Remember that the joy of the Lord is your strength. Love with all that you possess, feed your faith with the Word, come before God in humility, persevere, and be patient, for the Lord will surely bring it to pass!

> But they that wait upon the Lord shall renew their strength;
> they shall mount up with wings as eagles; they shall run, and
> not be weary; and they shall walk, and not faint.
>
> Isaiah 40:31 (KJV)

QUESTIONS FOR REFLECTION

Do you feel worthy of love? Do you feel
you are worthy of the love of Jesus?

Do you think you are too young or
too old for God to use you?

Do you feel unworthy to be used by God?

Are you guilty of thinking your calling is insignificant?

Have you specifically asked God to
show you someone in need?

Did you do everything you could to meet that need
or did you just simply say, I will pray about it?

Have you taken matters into your own hands
or are you still waiting for the promise?

Have you attempted to fill the void in your life
with things rather than Jesus Christ?

Are you allowing your past to stop or hinder you from accomplishing the will of God?

Does the man in your life love you as Christ loves the church?

Are you submissive to your spouse,
the way God commands it?

Did you realize when you and your spouse are
not in unity; it will hinder your prayers?

Do you use manipulation and control to get what you
want from your spouse, your children or others?

Is the way you dress and present yourself, pleasing to God or could it cause someone to sin?

Are you willing to fight for all that God
has for you and your loved ones?

Are you a lady of virtue, a pearl of great price and beauty?

PRAYER

Jesus,
I thank You that because of Your love and sacrifice I am
made worthy. I am worthy to be loved by You and those who
surround me. I have come to the realization that it does not
matter, whether I am young or old, rich or poor, free or in
bondage, single, married, divorced or widowed; I am still
valuable to Your kingdom. I fully understand that it does

not matter about my past or my present for You can and will change my life. Lord Jesus, use me as never before. Neither my past nor my present will stop me from accomplishing the will of God for my life. I will do my best not to belittle my calling ever again. For in my calling if I am obedient; You will judge it as success. Give me the love and compassion to seek out those who are in need and to help them with the best of my ability. Give me the strength, courage, faith, patience and perseverance to wait upon You for the promise. Do not allow me to take matters into my own hands. Keep me from searching for things to fill the void in my life rather than Jesus Christ? I thank you, Lord; by faith, my spouse loves me as Christ loves the church. Help me to be submissive to my spouse as God commands. Do not allow me to use control or manipulation for it is rebellion and witchcraft. May we stay in unity with each other and with God, so our prayers will be answered. I will present myself and dress in an appropriate manner so I will not cause someone else to fall into sin. I will fight for all that You love and fight against all that You hate. Help me to wage war for the salvation, healing, deliverance, protection and provision for my loved ones and for me. Do not allow the enemy to bring condemnation upon me because I have failed in some aspects of the Proverbs 31 woman; but help me to strive to be the best I can be. With Your strength I can be a virtuous woman; a pearl of great price and beauty. I give You all the praise, honor and glory. Amen.

You Are a Speaking Spirit

God created the world with Jesus and the presence of the Holy Spirit, and by the words, He spoke. In Genesis, it gave an account of how God spoke Creation into existence.

> In the beginning God created the heavens and the earth. And the earth was without form and void; and darkness was upon the face of the deep. And the Spirit of God (Holy Spirit) moved upon the face of the waters. And God said, Let there be light: and there was light. And God saw the light, that it was good: and God divided the light from the darkness.
>
> Genesis 1:1-4 (KJV)

Through these four scriptures, you will find a pattern, which God used to create everything. First, the Holy Spirit's presence was with God and Jesus; He spoke the thing He wanted to create, He saw what He created, and then He put the creation into action. The Bible tells us, "The words that I speak unto you, they are spirit, and they are life" (John 6:63, KJV).

At this point in time, you are probably thinking that was God! I do not possess that same power and authority. Yet, that is exactly what Satan wants you to believe; it is how he manages to keep us in bondage. On the contrary, you do have that power and authority if you believe it in your heart and confess it with your mouth. The

Word tells us we can do even greater things than Christ; which means we can do them in greater measure.

> Verily, Verily, I say unto you, He that believeth on me, the works that I do shall he do also; and greater works than these shall he do; because I go unto My Father.
>
> John 14:12 (KJV)

If you have the same spirit, your words have the same power of life, abundant life. Therefore, your words should be of faith.

> We having the same spirit of faith, according as it is written, I believed, and therefore have I spoken; we also believe, and therefore speak.
>
> 2 Corinthians 4:13 (KJV)

I am stepping on my own toes here, but I believe the following is absolutely true, "Yet ye have not, because ye ask not. Ye ask, and receive not, because ye ask amiss, that ye may consume it upon your lusts" (John 4:2-3, KJV). If we do not open our mouth and ask, or if it is not according to the word of God, then we will definitely not receive the things we need or desire. This tells me if we are not receiving, then we are not believing, asking, and confessing the things we should! Or we are not asking according to the Word of God.

The seed written about in the book of Luke is referring to the word of God. The only seeds from our mouth we should be sowing are God's words. Just take the time, right now, to think about the confessions you have made over your life and the lives of others, recently. Are they words of life or death, blessing or cursing, deliverance or bondage, encouragement or destruction?

We need to wise up and realize the power and authority we command with our tongues. The power we possess in our tongues can be used for good or evil. Which do you choose?

I call heaven and earth as witnesses today against you, that I have set before you life and death, blessing and cursing; therefore choose life, that both you and your descendants may live; that you may love the Lord your God; that you may obey His voice, and you may cling to Him, for He is your life and the length of your days; and that you may dwell in the land which the Lord swore to your fathers, to Abraham, Isaac, and Jacob, to give them.

Deuteronomy 30:19 (NKJV)

What you say is what you get! It does not matter whether you believe it or not. The saying still holds true today, and it is a spiritual law that cannot be broken. God has spiritual laws that work for both the just and the unjust. We have all wondered at times, why the ungodly seem to prosper, when we are just barely surviving. Though they may be ungodly, God's principles still work for them.

Our problem is we have been brainwashed into thinking we are supposed to have a poverty mentality. We are supposed to let the world walk all over us by being humble; and if we are sick, it is because God is trying to teach us something. Hogwash! We are supposed to be the healthiest, most prosperous people in the world. "Beloved, I pray that you may prosper in all things and be in health, just as your soul prospers" (3 John 2, NKJV).

And you shall remember the Lord your God, for it is He who gives you power to get wealth, that He may establish His covenant which He swore to your fathers, as it is this day.

Deuteronomy 8:18 (NKJV)

Now, if He did not intend for us to be healthy, wealthy, and cause us to prosper in all things, He would not have put it in the Word, nor would He have given us the power to get wealth. We are heirs to the throne, and joint heirs with Jesus Christ. Our heavenly Father is the Creator of all things; therefore, He has ownership of everything. We need to wake up out of our stupor, (dazed or unconscious state), and take back our inheritance.

A few years back, I did a teaching at our church, which I entitled, "Hung by the Tongue." It was a powerful, mind-opening lesson; but if we do not apply the principles, what good does it do us? Approximately five years ago, I came across a book named, *The Power of Your Words*, written by Don Gossett and E. W. Kenyon. I felt impressed by the spirit of God to read this book. I bought more copies and gave it to friends and co-workers, who in turn bought more copies and gave them away. This is an extremely powerful book, and I highly recommend that you read it.

Recently, I came across a book in my husband's collection and, to my amazement, it was titled, *Hung by the Tongue*. Francis P. Martin wrote this book, and I would recommend this book, as well. I believe these two books will give you great revelation.

The title on the cover of the book was written in rope-like letters, which had a hangman's noose hanging from it, and a man hanging from the noose. This really caught my eye because, in my teaching, I actually used a game we used to play when we were children called, "Hangman." The game consisted of drawing a gallows (frame for hanging). One person picks a word and then makes a line for each letter of the word; the opponent playing the game is supposed to guess a letter. If the opponent guesses a letter correctly, the letter is put into whatever space it belongs. However, if they guess incorrectly, a circle, representing the head is drawn in the rope that is hanging from the gallows. As the game continues, and you guess the letters incorrectly, the whole body will be drawn on the paper until you become the "hung man." If you get the letters correct and guess the word, then you will win the game. Such is the game of life, if you say the correct things, if you speak the word of God, then you win! If you say the incorrect things, and you speak what Satan speaks, you speak destruction and death, whether it be with your marriage, your children, prosperity, or health; you lose! What are you speaking? Which leads me to ask, what are you thinking, because the Word says out of the abundance of the heart, the mouth speaks?

The only way we will ever inherit what was bought and paid for by Jesus Christ is to have the Word abiding in us, believe the Word, and apply the Word by our confession.

> A man's stomach shall be satisfied from the fruit of his mouth; From the produce of his lips he shall be filled. Death and life are in the power of the tongue, and those who love it will eat its fruit.
>
> Proverbs 18:20-21 (NKJV)

It tells us in James 3 that the man who would be able to control his tongue would be considered a "perfect" man, though we all know there is only one "perfect one," and that is Jesus. We cannot always be perfect in our speech, but we should seriously guard our tongues. The only way to do that is to fill our hearts with the word of God.

> A good man out of the good treasure of his heart brings forth good; and an evil man out of the evil treasure of his heart brings forth evil. For out of the abundance of the heart his mouth speaks.
>
> Luke 6:45 (NKJV)

> In the beginning was the Word, and the Word was with God, and the Word was God. He was in the beginning with God. All things were made through Him, and without Him nothing was made. In Him was life, and the life was the light of men.
>
> John 1:1-4 (NKJV)

Therefore, we see there is life in the Word, which brings life to our words. The Word was with us in the beginning, and He will be with us throughout eternity. We only have victory over Satan when we speak the Word. "And they overcame him by the blood of the Lamb and by the word of their testimony" (Revelation 12:20, KJV).

Our words can set us free or keep us in bondage, give us life or death, blessing or cursing, health or sickness, prosperity or poverty, faith or fear. You can conquer Satan and all he brings against you by the words you speak. The Word says you are made more than a conqueror through Christ.

> Who shall separate us from the love of Christ? Shall tribulation, or distress, or persecution, or famine, or nakedness, or peril, or sword? As it is written, for thy sake we are killed all the day long; we are accounted as sheep for the slaughter. Nay, in all these things we are more than conquerors through Him that loved us.
>
> Romans 8:35-37 (KJV)

Again, I reiterate, God created the world with Jesus and the presence of the Holy Spirit and by the words, He spoke. You can also create your world, and the world of those around you, by the words you speak. More times than not, I have regretted not having the revelation of those words when I was raising my children. My prayer for you is that you will take power and authority over the words that are spoken over your life, your marriage, children, and grandchildren. Speak life, and do not allow anyone else to speak negatively over them, either.

Your words can be salvation or damnation. Salvation is received from confessing with our mouth that Jesus Christ is Lord. You can find this in Romans 10. Never will you have the good, the abundance; you will not be successful or prosperous, healthy or strong until you change your heart, your thoughts, and your words. As long as you speak poverty, sickness, and defeat, that is what you will continue to receive. Boldly declare the word of God is truth. Whatever God says about you and your situation is absolute truth!

As I said before, your words are living words. Once spoken, they are birthed into existence; in other words, they create the thing you said. I believe what takes place in the spiritual realm is this: When you speak something, there is a messenger ready to take those words and put them into action, whether the thing you spoke was good or evil. If it was good, the angel of God takes it and brings it forth. However, if you spoke evil, then the fallen angel of Satan takes charge of it and brings forth evil. That is why it is so important to guard our tongue!

Remember, I said you could speak things over other people. Approximately five years ago, I had a blood clot in my leg and could not walk without limping or favoring that leg. People began to tease me about it. One person, in particular, started calling me Chester and Festus (you know, from the show, *Gunsmoke*). He also used the nickname, "Crip". After reading the book, *Power of Your Words*, a righteous indignation rose up within me. The next time that person called me a name like that, I answered him, "If you call me anything, call me healed!" This person was completely shocked; but you know, he never called me by those names again, and he apologized. Shortly after that declaration of faith, I noticed the pain was gone and I was walking normally. Praise God! See what a statement of faith can accomplish!

Right now, I am battling sickness; that is why I say I am stepping on my own toes. Over the years, I have suffered many attacks against my body; but God has always healed me. For over six years, I have suffered with sinus and lung problems, with the medications causing other complications. The doctors diagnosed me with several things, such as COPD, asthma, and bronchitis, all of which I quickly rebuked in the name of Jesus. I have been anointed with oil and prayed over more times, than I could count. I have confessed the word of God over myself, scripture after scripture, but to no avail.

Have you ever had a "suddenly"? My "suddenly" came when I realized the words I was confessing. I would quote, "By His stripes, I am healed," but with the next breath, I would nullify that scripture without even realizing it. Example: "By His stripes I am healed," then when I would take a breath, I would say something like this, "It hurts when I breathe," or "I can't breathe." Granted, these things were reality; they were fact, but they are not truth. The truth is: I am healed! I cannot make a right confession, then a wrong confession and expect to see a manifestation of that healing. My confession of pain, weakness, or shortness of breath only served, to make the disease stronger. It is the same with anything in your life. Learn to make the right confession and not cancel it with the next word out of your mouth. Confess the positive, not the negative!

Sometimes, we would fair better if we would just keep our mouths shut. My mother used to tell me if I could not say something good, then I should not say anything at all. There is a lot more wisdom and truth to this statement than we realize.

> He who has knowledge spares his words, and a man of understanding is of a calm spirit. Even a fool is counted wise when he holds his peace; when he shuts his lips, he is considered perceptive.
>
> Proverbs 17:27-28 (NKJV)

> Do not be rash with your mouth, And let not your heart utter anything hastily before God. For God is in heaven and you on earth; therefore let your words be few. For a dream comes through much activity, and a fool's voice is known by his many words.
>
> Ecclesiastes 5:2-3 (NKJV)

If you have difficulty taming your tongue, remember, once spoken, your words cannot be recaptured, and you will be held accountable for them. We find that our words can even be counted as sin. David said it like this:

> I said, "I will take heed to my ways that I sin not with my tongue: I will keep my mouth with a bridle, while the wicked is before me."
>
> Psalm 39:1 (KJV)

When my husband, Tom, and I have a difference of opinion, he gets upset because most of the time, I tend to clam up. He has made the statement that I do it to punish him. That is not true; I try very hard to be extremely careful with what I say. Unfortunately, I do not always succeed. As I said before, no matter how hard you try or how much you apologize, you cannot retrieve those words, nor can you stop the damage those words will cause. The person that derived the little saying, "Sticks and stones may break my bones; but words will never hurt me," had absolutely no clue as to what they were saying. This statement could not be further from the truth. The truth is they cut like a jagged knife, meaning they take a long time to heal. In addition, I try to be silent because I do not want to have to repent for words said in anger or bring judgment upon myself.

Jesus speaks a lot about accountability; listen to what He says in Matthew:

> But I say unto you, that every idle word that men shall speak, they shall give account thereof in the Day of Judgment. For by the words thou shalt be justified, and by thy words thou shalt be condemned.
>
> Matthew 12:36-37 (KJV)

David is talking about speaking poems, songs, and praises unto the Lord when he said, "My tongue is the pen of a ready writer" (Psalm 45:1, KJV). I believe our tongues are pens, also, when it comes to the things we say. We are actually writing our futures, creating our worlds, by the words we speak. Right after Jesus cursed the fig tree and it died from the root, He made the remark as follows:

> Have faith in God. For verily I say unto you, That whosoever shall say unto this mountain, Be thou removed, and be thou cast into the sea; and shall not doubt in his heart, but shall believe that those things which he saith shall come to pass; he shall have whatsoever he saith.
>
> Mark 11:22-23 (KJV)

That tells us we can actually frame our lives and the lives of others by our speech, and nothing is impossible to those that believe.

Remember, when Jesus Christ died at Calvary, we became eligible for salvation, healing, deliverance, protection and provision, the totality of abundant life. However, we do not receive those things until we believe it and confess it with our mouth.

> The heart of the wise teaches his mouth, and addeth learning to his lips. Pleasant words are as a honeycomb, sweet to the soul and health to the bones.
>
> Proverbs 16:23-24 (KJV)

Let us teach our mouths to be full of wisdom, life, love, compassion, encouragement, and healing. Begin to create your world by speaking the Word of God, hold fast to your confession until your hopes, dreams, and desires come to pass. Especially, remember these two vital points: What are you thinking and speaking? Believe it or not, it does not change the fact that "you are a speaking spirit"!

QUESTIONS FOR REFLECTION

Are you aware you are a speaking spirit?

Did you realize that your words have the power and authority to create?

Think back for a moment and analyze the confessions you have made in the past; were they positive or negative?

How have the confessions manifested in your life and the lives of others?

Honestly, have you been hung by your tongue?

What are you thinking, for out of the heart the mouth speaks?

What are you speaking; is it life or death, blessing or cursing, abundance or lack, deliverance or bondage, or health or sickness?

Specifically, what are you speaking over your spouse and your children?

Are you allowing others to speak negatively into your life or the lives of your loved ones?

Normally, do you guard your tongue or say the first thing, which comes to your mind?

Do you understand that you will be held accountable for every idle word, which comes out of your mouth?

PRAYER

Father,

Give me the revelation that I am a speaking spirit and that my words have the power and authority to create. Reveal to me the times when my words have wrecked havoc upon my life or the lives of my loved ones. Also, show me the areas where my words have brought in the blessings of God. Grant me the strength not to bring death, destruction, theft, sickness, or lack into our lives. Give me a clear and balanced mind so I may speak correctly in accordance with Your Word. Help me to speak words of life and encouragement instead of death and condemnation, especially over my family. Reveal to me how to speak health and prosperity into every area of our lives. I refuse to allow the enemy or others to speak negatively over us. I will guard my tongue and think about things before I say them. I understand that I will be held accountable for every idle word I say, and I pray that I will be justified, not condemned on the Day of Judgment. In Jesus name, I pray. Amen.

Promises, Promises

*H*ow many times has someone promised you something that never came to pass? For that matter, how many promises have you broken to yourself or someone else? How many times have you broken promises to God? Like most of us, I am quite sure you have failed more times than you could count. I have always tried to uphold the promises I made but at times have failed, miserably.

Now, this is not to bring condemnation on you. We have all failed at our promise keeping skills, at one time or another. Nevertheless, I know a "Promise Keeper" Who will never fail or come short on His promises. Not only does He keep His promises, but also He does more than you could ever think or imagine. There is my favorite scripture again:

> Now unto Him that is able to do exceeding abundantly above all that we ask or think, according to the power that worketh in us.
>
> Ephesians 3:20 (KJV)

In addition, to the "exceeding abundantly above all," He also makes sure He is there right on time. In other words, He is never late! Be honest, you could not ask for more than that, could you? We serve an awesome God!

Reportedly, there are over three thousand promises in the Bible. I have also heard there is a scripture on fear for every day of the year. Whether or not this is true, I am not certain, but feel these two statements are probably true. Regardless, whether this is factual or not, I do know there is a scripture for every situation you might encounter in your lifetime. It does not matter what you are facing, you can find comfort and peace in scripture. If you are searching for answers, the first place you should look is in the word of God. Unfortunately, we tend to call our friends, cry woe is me, and ask them for opinions, when we should be seeking God's face, first!

Who knows the temptations and the sufferings we go through better than Jesus Christ? Absolutely, no one! He knows the beginning from the end; He suffered and was tempted and tried to a much greater degree than we could ever imagine.

> For we have not an high priest (Jesus Christ) which cannot be touched with the feeling of our infirmities; but was in all points tempted like as we are, yet without sin. Let us therefore come boldly unto the throne of grace that we may obtain mercy, and find grace to help in time of need.
> Hebrews 4:15-16 (KJV)

He knows your future, He knows His plans for you, He knows your innermost feelings and thoughts, and furthermore, He knows how to calm and disperse your storms. So, why would you not go to Him first? It plainly tells us to go boldly to the throne of grace.

I am not saying we should not seek counsel and wisdom from others. The Word tells us there is much wisdom in counsel. "Pride leads to arguments; those who take advice are wise" (Proverbs 13:10, NLT).

> People who despise advice will find themselves in trouble; those who respect it will succeed. The advice of the wise is a

life-giving fountain; those who accept it avoid the snares of death.

Proverbs 14:13-14 (NLT)

The point I am trying to make is seek God, first. Let the others confirm what you believe was revealed to you in the Word or through prayer. After all, "true wisdom" comes from God.

God's Word is inundated with powerful promises on salvation, healing, deliverance, protection and provision for every area of your life. They are all yours, just for the asking! They have been made readily available for you through the cross. The promises of God are provided for us; they are gifts. All we have to do is ask, believe, and receive them. Trust in God to deliver the promise in His time, not yours. Sometimes we tend to get impatient; but hold to the promise, He will surely bring it to pass! Do everything in your power to prepare for the promise, and then watch God perform it. All God's promises are "yes" and "amen" to a true believer!

How would you feel if you bought your child a gift, and you were reaching out to give it to them, but they refused to take it and just walked away? Oh, how it must hurt God deeply. Yet, we have done this to Him repeatedly. When are we going to accept what He has already bought and paid for, what He has so freely given?

In the following pages, you will find a few of the promises of God. I found these scriptures to be my source of strength, in order to hold on to, and obtain the promises of God as a "lady in waiting." I am confident in the word of God, and that these promises will be a source of strength for you, also.

As you read the following scriptures, make them personal to you and your situation or need. Example: "For God has not given me (or your name) the spirit of fear; but of power, and of love, and of a sound mind." Again, I say, you are a speaking spirit!

Children

Our children are very precious gifts from God. He has entrusted them to us for a time and a season, to love, nurture, guide, and train them in the ways of the Lord. We are to protect and shield them from the ungodly things of this world. These scriptures helped me when I was praying for my children, raising my children, and while I prayed that they would turn back to the ways of the Lord.

> For this child I prayed, and the Lord has granted me my petition, which I asked of Him. Therefore, I also have lent him to the Lord; as long as he lives he shall be lent to the Lord.
>
> 1 Samuel 1:27-28 (NKJV)

> Train up a child in the way he should go, and when he is old he will not depart from it.
>
> Proverbs 22:6 (NKJV)

> Fear not for I am with you; I will bring your descendants from the east, and gather you from the west; I will say to the north, "Give them up!" And to the south, "Do not keep them back!" Bring My sons from afar and My daughters from the ends of the earth.
>
> Isaiah 43:5-6 (NKJV)

> The rod (discipline) and rebuke give wisdom, but a child left to himself brings shame to his mother." "Correct your son and he will give you rest. Yes, he will give delight to your soul.
>
> Proverbs 29:15, 17 (NKJV)

> And you, fathers, do not provoke your children to wrath, but bring them up in the training and admonition of the Lord.
>
> Ephesians 6:4 (NKJV)

> Behold, children are a heritage from the Lord, The fruit of the womb is a reward. Like arrows in the hand of a warrior,

So are the children of one's youth. Happy is the man who has his quiver full of them; they shall not be ashamed.

Psalm 127:3-5 (NKJV)

If you then, being evil, know how to give good gifts to your children, how much more will your Father who is in heaven give good things to those who ask Him.

Matthew 7:11 (NKJV)

But Jesus said, "Let the little children come to Me, and do not forbid them; for of such is the kingdom of heaven."

Matthew 19:14 (NKJV)

He will love you, bless you, and multiply you; He will also bless the fruit of your womb and the fruit of your land, your grain and your new wine and your oil, the increase of your cattle and the offspring of your flock, in the land of which He swore to your fathers to give to you. You shall be blessed above all peoples; there shall not be a male or female barren among you or among your livestock.

Deuteronomy 7:13-14 (NKJV)

And it shall come to pass in the last days, says God that I will pour out My Spirit on all flesh; your sons and your daughters shall prophesy.

Acts 2:17 (NKJV)

Before I formed you in the womb I knew you; before you were born I sanctified you; I ordained you a prophet to the nations.

Jeremiah 1:5 (NKJV)

Desires

Many are the desires of the flesh; but a "lady in waiting" will have godly desires. Not only will she have godly desires, but she will endeavor to put God first. Seek first the kingdom of God and His righteousness, and all these things will be added unto you. If you are not self-seeking, if you will allow God to bring your desires to you, then He will, in turn, give you the best, He has to offer. After all, He knows more about what will make you happy and content than you know yourself. If you will allow God to put the right desires in your heart then He will gladly bring them to you.

Lord You have heard the desire of the humble; You will prepare their heart; You will cause Your ear to hear.

Psalm 10:17 (NKJV)

You have given him his heart's desire, and have not withheld the request of his lips. Selah. For You meet him with the blessings of goodness; You set a crown of pure gold upon his head. He asked life from You, and You gave it to him—

Psalm 21:2-4 (NKJV)

Delight thyself also in the Lord, and He shall give you the desires of your heart. Commit your way to the Lord, Trust also in Him, and He shall bring it to pass.

Psalm 37:4-5 (NKJV)

The Lord upholds all who fall and rises up all who are bowed down. The eyes of all look expectantly to You, and You give them their food in due season. You open Your hand, and satisfy the desire of every living thing. The Lord is righteous in all His ways, Gracious in all His works. The Lord is near to all who call upon Him in truth. He will fulfill the desire of those who fear Him; He also will hear their cry and save them.

Psalm 145:14-19 (NKJV)

And the desire of the righteous will be granted.

Proverbs 10:24 (NKJV)

The soul of a lazy man desires, and has nothing; but the soul of the diligent shall be made rich.

Proverbs 13:4 (NKJV)

Hope deferred makes the heart sick, but when the desire comes, it is a tree of life.

Proverbs 13:12 (NKJV)

Pursue love and desire spiritual gifts, but especially that you may prophesy.

1 Corinthians 14:1 (NKJV)

Fear

Many things plague our lives; but fear is one of the most effective tools Satan uses against us. We have all experienced fear at one time or another. Through fear, Satan can and will paralyze every avenue of our lives, if we allow him to do so. Remember this: If we are in fear, we are not in faith! "And He said to them, why are ye so fearful? How is it that ye have no faith?" (Mark 4:40, NKJV)

Fear is mentioned numerous times in the Bible. Repeatedly, God tells us not to fear, except when it is the fear (reverence) of the Lord. There are too many to list them all; but here are a few of my favorites:

For God has not given us the spirit of fear; but of power, and of love, and of a sound mind.

2 Timothy 1:7 (NKJV)

For the Lord your God will hold your right hand, saying to you, "Fear not, I will help thee.

Isaiah 41:13 (NKJV)

When you lie down, you will not be afraid; yes, you will lie down, and your sleep will be sweet.

Proverbs 3:24 (NKJV)

Yea, though I walk through the valley of the shadow of death, I will fear no evil; for You are with me; Your rod and Your staff, they comfort me.

Psalm 23:4 (NKJV)

And do not fear those who kill the body, but cannot kill the soul. But rather fear Him (God) Who is able to destroy both soul and body in hell. Are not two sparrows sold for a copper coin? And not one of them falls to the ground apart from your Father's will. But the very hairs of your head are all numbered. Do not fear therefore, you are of more value than many sparrows.

Matthew 10:28-31 (NKJV)

Do not be afraid. Stand still, and see the salvation of the Lord, which He will accomplish for you today. For the Egyptians (enemies) whom you see today, you see again no more forever. The Lord will fight for you, and you shall hold your peace.

Exodus 14:13-14 (NKJV)

You shall not be afraid of the terror by night, Nor of the arrow that flies by day, Nor of the pestilence that walks in darkness, nor of the destruction that lays waste at noonday. A thousand may fall at your side, and ten thousand at your right hand; But it shall not come near you.

Psalm 91:5-7 (NKJV)

Only fear the Lord, and serve Him in truth with all your heart; for consider what great things He has done for you.

1 Samuel 12:24 (NKJV)

But now, thus says the Lord, Who created you, O Jacob, And He Who formed you, O Israel: Fear not for I have redeemed you; you are Mine. When you pass through the waters, I will be with you; And through the rivers, they shall not overflow you. When you walk through the fire, you shall not be burned, Nor shall the flame scorch you. For I Am the Lord your God, The holy one of Israel, your Savior.

Isaiah 43:1-3 (NKJV)

The Lord is my light and my salvation; Whom shall I fear? The Lord is the strength of my life; Of whom shall I be afraid? When the wicked came against me, To eat up my flesh, My enemies and foes, They stumbled and fell. Though an army may encamp against me, in this I will be confident. One thing I have desired of the Lord, That will I seek: That I may dwell in the house of the Lord, All the days of my life, To behold the beauty of the Lord, And to inquire in His temple. For in the time of trouble He shall hide me in His pavilion; In the secret place of His tabernacle He shall hide me; He shall set me high upon a rock.

Psalm 27:1-5 (NKJV)

Healing

My dependence has been upon Jesus to heal my loved ones or me many times throughout my life. He was always there to heal and comfort.

During this particular time in my life, there is sickness and pain that plagues my body. Nevertheless, sickness and pain are only names. The "truth" of the matter is I am healed and made whole in the name of Jesus. The Word tells me that every name has to bow at the name of Jesus, and by His stripes, I am healed!

You are healed, also. Your healing was "paid in full" on the cross. All you have to do is accept the gift He has already purchased on your behalf. Receive healing in every area of your life, now, in the name of Jesus.

But He was wounded for our transgressions, He was bruised for our iniquities; The chastisement of our peace was upon Him, and by His stripes we are healed.

Isaiah 53:5 (NKJV)

Heal me, Oh Lord, and I shall be healed; Save me, And I shall be saved.

Jeremiah 17:14 (NKJV)

For I will restore health to you, And heal you of your wounds, says the Lord, Because they called you an outcast saying: This is Zion; no one seeks her.

Jeremiah 30:17 (NKJV)

But to you who fear My name, the sun of righteousness shall arise, with healing in His wings.

Malachi 4:2 (NKJV)

And Jesus went about all Galilee, teaching in their synagogues, preaching the gospel of the kingdom, and healing all kinds of sickness and all kinds of disease among the people. Then His fame went throughout all Syria; and they brought to Him all sick people who were afflicted with various diseases and torments, and those who were demon-possessed, epileptics, and paralytics; and He healed them.

Matthew 4:23-24 (NKJV)

And the whole multitude sought to touch Him, for power went out from Him and healed them all.

Luke 6:19 (NKJV)

And He said to her, "Daughter, be of good cheer, your faith has made you well (whole). Go in peace."

Luke 8:48 (NKJV)

God anointed Jesus of Nazareth with the Holy Spirit and with power, who went about doing good and healing all who were oppressed by the devil, for God was with Him.

Acts 10:38 (NKJV)

Is anyone among you suffering? Let him pray. Is anyone cheerful? Let him sing psalms. Is anyone among you sick? Let him call for the elders of the church, and let them pray over him, anointing him with oil in the name of the Lord. And the prayer of faith will save the sick, and the Lord will raise him up. And if he commits sins, he will be forgiven. Confess your trespasses to one another, and pray for one another, that you may be healed. The effective fervent prayer of a righteous man avails much.

James 5:13-16 (NKJV)

Who Himself bore our sins in His own body on the tree, that we, having died to sins, might live for righteousness—by Whose stripes you were healed.

1 Peter 2:24 (NKJV)

Loneliness

Loneliness has a way of isolating you, even when you are not alone. It does not always mean you are by yourself. It could mean the lack of support or encouragement.

As I said earlier, I have been in places where I isolated myself and places where someone else isolated me. Believe me, it is not a good feeling when you are locked in a room, where there is no escape. Whether it is by your hand or by another, remember one of Satan's devices is to divide and conquer. It is at those times you really need to seek the presence of the Holy Spirit. He is the only comforter you have to talk to, the only one you have to rely on, and your only protection. The Holy Spirit was the one Who gave the mercy and the grace for me to make it through those trying times. He can be there for you, also, if you allow Him.

Being single or married has no bearing on whether you will be lonely or not. Most women think if they could just find someone to marry, they would not be lonely, anymore. This is just not true! I have been lonely, while I was married, and I have been lonely, when I was single.

Of course, this is just my opinion; but, for me, it was the worst kind of loneliness, when I was married. When you are married and your spouse chooses not to spend time with you, it is worse than not having anyone at all.

There are ladies out there that would rather be with someone who is abusive, in one form or another, than to be alone. Ladies, you are not only hurting yourself, but also the people who genuinely care about you. Especially, if there are children involved!

Set yourself apart for a while. Set yourself apart for the Holy Spirit. Let the Comforter come in and heal your life before you jump back into another relationship. Let the Holy Spirit be your husband for a season, so that He can bring you the man who has been chosen by God.

(For the Lord your God is a merciful God), He will not forsake you nor destroy you, nor forget the covenant of your fathers which He swore to them.
Deuteronomy 4:31 (NKJV)

Be strong and of good courage, do not fear nor be afraid of them, for the Lord your God, He is the one, Who goes with you. He will not leave you nor forsake you.
Deuteronomy 31:6 (NKJV)

When my father and mother forsake me, Then the Lord will take care of me.
Psalm 27:10 (NKJV)

I have been young, and now am old; Yet I have not seen the righteous forsaken, Nor his descendants begging bread.

Psalm 37:25 (NKJV)

I, the Lord, will hear them; I, the God of Israel, will not forsake them.

Isaiah 41:17 (NKJV)

Do not fear, for you will not be ashamed; Neither be disgraced, for you will not be put to shame; For you will forget the shame of your youth, And will not remember the reproach of your widowhood anymore. For your Maker is your Husband, The Lord of Hosts is His name; And your Redeemer is the Holy One of Israel; He is called the God of the whole earth.

Isaiah 54:4-5 (NKJV)

You shall no longer be termed, forsaken, nor shall your land any more be termed, desolate.

Isaiah 62:1 (NKJV)

If you love Me, keep My commandments. And I will pray the Father, and He will give you another helper (comforter), that He may abide with you forever—the Spirit of truth, whom the world cannot receive, because it neither sees Him nor knows Him; but you know Him, for He dwells with you, and will be in you.

John 14:16-18 (NKJV)

But the helper, the Holy Spirit, Whom the Father will send in My name, He will teach you all things, and bring to your remembrance all things that I said to you.

John 14:26 (NKJV)

We are hard-pressed on every side, yet not crushed; we are perplexed, but not in despair; persecuted, but not forsaken; struck down, but not destroyed—.

2 Corinthians 4:8-9 (NKJV)

Let your conduct be without covetousness; be content with such things as you have. For He Himself has said, "I will never leave you nor forsake you." So we may say: "The Lord is my helper; I will not fear. What can man do to me?"

Hebrews 13:5-6 (NKJV)

Marriage

Let me first say that God instituted the union of marriage. It is God's representation of the relationship between God and Israel and of Jesus as the husband of the Church, with the Church as His bride.

God joined the first couple, Adam and Eve, as husband and wife. Notice God made the choice for Adam. He did not give Adam a choice between several women, nor did He give Adam a choice between a man and a woman. God chose the best mate suited for Adam. Eve was handpicked from the rib of Adam, not to be above or beneath him, but to be by his side.

The first command God gave Adam and Eve was: "Multiply and fill the earth and subdue it" (Genesis 1:28, NLT). Only a man and a woman can multiply themselves!

God's plan for an ideal marriage was one man and one woman for a lifetime. Man is the one who changed from one woman to many, in order that they would have as many male descendants as possible to carry on their name. I personally believe there were other issues involved in their theory of multiple wives and concubines, but we will not go there!

I realize in today's world, it takes a strong determined commitment to stay married until death do you part. Nevertheless, with God's help, it is possible. The problem is that people do not take their commitments and their vows seriously. They think, oh well, if it does not work out the way they want it to; they will just get a divorce. That is the wrong attitude! It is a selfish attitude.

Unfortunately, many marriages are based on lust, not love. That is why we need to let Jesus heal all our wounds from past relationships, seek a husband/wife relationship with God; then, and only then, ask God to send your earthly husband. In my opinion, choosing a spouse is the second most important decision you will ever make. Therefore, make sure he is God-sent!

And the Lord God caused a deep sleep to fall upon Adam, and he slept; and He took one of his ribs, and closed up the flesh instead thereof. And the rib, which the Lord God had taken from man, made He a woman, and brought her unto the man. And Adam said, This is now bone of my bones, and flesh of my flesh: she shall be called Woman, because she was taken out of man. Therefore shall a man leave his father and his mother, and shall cleave unto his wife: and they shall be one flesh.

Genesis 2:21-24 (KJV)

And they twain (two) shall be one flesh: so then they shall be no more twain, but one flesh. What therefore God hath joined together let no man put asunder (separate into pieces).

Mark 10:8-9 (KJV)

And the women who hath a husband that believeth not, and if he be pleased to dwell with her, let her not leave him. For the unbelieving husband is sanctified by the wife. But if the unbelieving depart, let him depart.

1 Corinthians 7:13-15 (KJV)

Wives submit yourselves unto your own husbands, as unto the Lord. For the husband is the head of the wife, even as Christ is the head of the Church: and He is the savior of the body. Therefore as the Church is subject unto Christ, so let the wives be to their own husbands in everything.

Ephesians 5:22-24 (KJV)

And the wife sees that she reverences her husband.

Ephesians 5:33 (KJV)

Marriage is honorable in all, and the bed undefiled: but whoremongers and adulterers God will judge.

Hebrews 13:4 (KJV)

Unmarried

Whether you are single, divorced or widowed, God has a word and a plan for you. Take this precious time to become intimate with God. This is the most important relationship you could possibly have. Spend time with the person who knows you better than anyone else. Search out the plans He has in store for you. You will be thankful you did!

Remember this: If you have, been involved sexually with a person, whether you were married to them or not, you have a soul tie with that person. You are spiritually connected to them, whether you realize it or not. The Bible states that we become one with that person (found in 1 Corinthians 6). A sexual sin is different in nature, because it involves your body. Your body is supposed to be the temple of God. Most people do not realize the repercussions of these actions. In order that you have a healthy relationship with your future spouse, you need to sever the soul tie with the person or persons involved. In other words, you need to repent, ask for forgiveness, receive forgiveness and, through the Spirit, give their spirit back to them then take your spirit back from that person.

You are a whole person with or without a man in your life. Keep yourself pure before the Lord, and allow Him to bring your spouse to you. Wait patiently on the Lord, and He will give you the desires of your heart.

I say therefore to the unmarried and widows, It is good for them if they abide even as I (Paul). But if they cannot contain, let them marry: for it is better to marry than to burn.

1 Corinthians 7:8-9 (KJV)

The unmarried woman careth for the things of the Lord, that she may be holy both in body and in spirit.

1 Corinthians 7:34 (KJV)

Don't you know that those who do wrong will have no share in the Kingdom of God? Don't fool yourselves. Those who indulge in sexual sin, who are idol worshipers, adulterers, male prostitutes, homosexuals, thieves, greedy people, drunkards, abusers, and swindlers—none of these will have a share in the kingdom of God.

1 Corinthians 6: 9-10 (NLT)

But our bodies were not made for sexual immorality. They were made for the Lord, and the Lord cares about our bodies.

1 Corinthians 6:13 (NLT)

Run away from sexual sin! No other sin so clearly affects the body as this one does. For sexual immorality is a sin against your own body. Or do you know that your body is the temple of the Holy Spirit, who lives in you and was given to you by God? You do not belong to yourself, for God bought you with a high price (Jesus Christ). So you must honor God with your body.

1 Corinthians 6:18-20 (NLT)

How can a young person stay pure? By obeying Your Word and following its rules, I have tried my best to find You— don't let me wonder from Your commands. I have hidden Your Word in my heart, that I might not sin against You.

Psalm 119:9-11 (NLT)

I weep with grief; encourage me by Your Word. Keep me from lying to myself; give me the privilege of knowing Your law. I have chosen to be faithful; I have determined to live by Your laws. I cling to Your decrees. Lord, don't let me put to shame! If you will help me, I will run to follow Your commands.

Psalm 119:28-32 (NLT)

In closing, please remember God's promises are true; they are "Yes" and "Amen"! The rainbow is a symbol of the promises He gave us. It is a reminder that He keeps His Word from the beginning to the end. I encourage you to be a "lady in waiting" for the promises of God"!

God is not a man, that He should lie, Nor a son of man, that He should repent. Has He said, and will He not do? Or has He spoken, and will He not make it good?

Numbers 23:19 (NKJV)

For as the rain comes down, and the snow from heaven, And do not return there, But water the earth, And make it bring forth and bud, That it may give seed to the sower, and bread to the eater, So shall My Word be that goes forth from My mouth; It shall not return to Me void, But it shall accomplish what I please. And it shall prosper in the thing for which I sent it.

Isaiah 55:10-11 (NKJV)

QUESTIONS FOR REFLECTION

Do you sincerely seek the kingdom of God first or do you seek the opinions of others first?

Do you seek godly council and compare it with what God said before you take their advice?

Have you truly put your trust in God to fulfill the promises in your life?

Are you training your children in the ways of the Lord?

Have you given your children over to God's care?

What are your goals, dreams and desires and
do you believe God can fulfill them?

In what ways are you fearful?

Do you truly believe that Jesus can and will heal you?

What or who is the source of loneliness or isolation?

What do you intend to do concerning the loneliness or isolation?

Would you really rather be with someone who is abusive than to be alone?

Are you hurting others by your actions,
especially your children?

Did God choose your spouse or did you?

Is your marriage based on love, trust and commitment?

Is God the key partner in your marriage?

God's knowledge and love for you is supe-
rior to anyone else; therefore, I ask you, are
you spending intimate time with Him?

Have you been involved in sexual sin? If so, have
you repented and asked for forgiveness?

Have you broken all soul ties, by calling out their names in prayer, and releasing their spirits back to them, breaking all ties spiritually, physically, and emotionally?

PRAYER

Father God,

I come into Your presence with thanksgiving and praise. I repent of all my sin, I ask forgiveness, and I receive forgiveness. If I have any ungodly soul ties, I call them out by name. I declare that I take back my spirit from them, and I release their spirit back to them; I sever all ties with them spiritually, physically, mentally, emotionally and financially. In the name of Jesus, according to Matthew 18:18-19, I bind up; I forbid and decree that all death, destruction and theft, all sickness, disease, infirmity, and pestilence, all poverty and lack, and every evil or negative thing are utterly destroyed. I furthermore decree and declare that all their effects are destroyed, in my life, in the lives of all my loved ones, and their loved ones. I curse their roots, their fruits, and their seeds. I, also, bind up every plan of the enemy and every negative word spoken over my life or the lives of my loved ones. Now that they are bound up, in the name of Jesus, I cast them into the sea of forgetfulness. God, You said my sins would be remembered no more. The blood of Jesus Christ covers my sins. Now, that all evil works are bound and destroyed in our lives, I pray, Father, that I have the mind of Christ and the heart of God. I pray my eyes of understanding are opened. You will cause the scales to fall from my eyes so that I may see clearly, spiritually, and physically. Cause me to know and understand who I am in Christ Jesus. Reveal to others and me that I am truly a "lady in waiting" and a "daughter of the King"! My ears will hear Your voice clearly above all others, especially the voice of the enemy or the voice of the flesh. Father, You said Your children know Your voice. Help me, Lord, to hear and obey Your voice, quickly. My hearing is made whole, both spiritually and physically. I pray You will shut the mouth of Satan and of those who speak against my loved ones or me. Teach me when to speak and when to be silent. My mouth will sing and speak Your Word. I confess with my mouth and believe in my heart that Jesus Christ is Lord of my life. With my tongue, I will testify of Your goodness and mercy. Let the words of my mouth edify the Trinity and the body of Christ. Let my mouth speak life, encouragement and healing. Help me to frame my world through my thoughts, words, and my actions, when they are in agreement with Your Word. Bless my hands that they might serve You all the days of my life. May they reach out to others in love and service. I pray my hands will be instruments of salvation, deliverance, healing, protection, provision, and restoration. May they be empowered with Your anointing. In other words, allow my hands to be an extension of the hands of Jesus Christ! Guide my every footstep, for You said the footsteps of the righteous are ordered by the Lord. Guide my pathways in life and bless me as I endeavor to do Your will. Everywhere, I put my feet, Lord, give me the territory. I thank You that my family, friends, and loved ones will be saved, and will fulfill the call of God upon their lives, right down to the last generation. Thank You for providing health, wealth, prosperity, and success in every area of our lives. You are El Shadai in our lives, "the God of more than enough," the God of abundance and overflow! I ask for a supernatural anointing of wisdom, knowledge, and understanding. I thank You for love, joy, peace, mercy, grace, and strength. Most of all, I thank You for my Lord and Savior, Jesus Christ. Have Your way in our lives. Prayerfully, I ask the Father to grant these petitions in the precious Name of Jesus. Amen and Amen.

Afterword

During the course of this writing, God has impressed upon me to start "Lady In Waiting Ministries". It is my heart's desire that we will be able to distribute books to hurting women who may be incarcerated, in shelters for battered women, or who just simply cannot afford to purchase a book.

I trust this book has ministered to you in at least one way, if not many. If this ministry has touched you, we challenge and encourage you to minister to the lives of other women who desperately need a touch from God.

Reach down deep within yourself to help others. You can purchase a book to give to someone of your choice, or you may purchase a book through this ministry; which will be distributed to a facility for women.

We thank you for your loving support. May God bless you, abundantly!

Lady In Waiting Ministries
288 Williams Road
Barney, Georgia 31625
Email: t2hiers@ yahoo.com
http://ladyinwaiting.tateauthor.com